THE EDUCATION
OF THE CHILD

[XXV]

FOUNDATIONS OF WALDORF EDUCATION

RUDOLF STEINER

The Education
of the Child

and Early Lectures on Education

⊘ Anthroposophic Press

Copyright © Anthroposophic Press, 1996

Published by Anthroposophic Press
RR 4, Box 94 A-1, Hudson, N.Y. 12534

The essay "The Education of the Child in the Light of Spiritual Science," translated by George and Mary Adams, appeared originally in German in the journal *Lucifer-Gnosis* (nr. 33), 1907, under the title "Die Erzieuhung des Kindes vom Geschictspunkte der Geisteswissenschaft." It is included in vol. 34 of the Collected Works of Rudolf Steiner, published by Rudolf Steiner Verlag, Dornach, Switzerland, 1987. The lecture "Teaching from a Foundation of Spiritual Insight," translated by Robert Lathe and Nancy Whittaker, is included in *Ursprungsimpulse der Geisteswissenschaft*, vol. 96, as "Erziehungspraxis auf der Grundlage spiritueller Erkenntnis"; the lecture "Education in the Light of Spiritual Science," translated by Rita Stebbing, appeared as "Die Erziehung des Kindes vom Standpunkt der Geisteswissenschaft"; and the lecture "Education and Spiritual Science," translated by Rita Stebbing, appeared as "Schulfragen vom Standpunkt der Geisteswissenschaft" in *Die Erkenntnis des Ubersinnlichen in unserer Zeit*, vol. 55; the lecture "Interests, Talent, and Education," translated by Robert Lathe and Nancy Whittaker, is included in *Antworten der eisteswissenschaft auf die grossen Fragen des Daseins*, vol. 60, as "Anlage, Begabung und Erziehung des Menschen," all of which are in the Collected Works of Rudolf Steiner, published by Rudolf Steiner Verlag, Dornach, Switzerland, 1987. The lecture "Interests, Talents, and Educating Children," translated by Robert Lathe and Nancy Whittaker, appeared originally in the magazine *Die Menschenschule*, vol. 31 (nr. 6),1957 and vol. 48 (nr.1), 1974.

Library of Congress Cataloging-in-Publication Data

Steiner, Rudolf, 1861–1925.
    [Selections. English. 1996]
    The education of the child and early lectures on education / Rudolf Steiner.
       p. cm. — (Foundations of Waldorf education ; 25)
    Three lectures and an essay translated from the German.
    Includes bibliographical references and index.
    ISBN 0-88010-414-7 (paper)
    1. Education—Philosophy. 2. Anthroposophy. 3. Education—Experimental methods. I. Title. II. Title: Education of the Child III. Series.
LB775.S7S7413   1996
370'.1—dc20   96-15013
                                                                       CIP

10 9 8 7 6 5 4 3 2 1

All rights reserved. No part of this book may be reproduced in any form without the written permission of the publisher, except for brief quotations embodied in critical reviews and articles.

Printed in the United States of America

CONTENTS

The publisher wishes to acknowledge the inspiration
and support of Connie and Robert Dulaney

❖ ❖ ❖

INTRODUCTION

by Christopher Bamford

One of the keys to Rudolf Steiner's ability to penetrate and accomplish so much in so many different fields lies in the fact that, in addition to possessing profound philosophical, spiritual, and mystical abilities, he was both scientifically trained and an eminently *practical person*. All his life, Rudolf Steiner was a "doer," able to take care of himself and those around him. He could size up any task or situation that seemed to call for a response and then act so as to bring it to a successful conclusion in the world. Thus, though endowed with tremendous innate capacities, Steiner was also in many ways a self-made man. Indeed, it was this combination of practicality and hard work together with a rich natural spiritual endowment that enabled him to achieve his mission.

Outwardly and socially at least, the circumstances of his birth did not apparently augur well for one destined to play a world-historical role. He was born in 1861 in Kraljevec, a small railroad town on the way to Trieste in the hinterland of the Austro-Hungarian empire—on the border between Hungary and Croatia. Eighteen months later, his father, who worked for the railroad, was transferred from Kraljevec, first to Mödling, near Vienna, and then to Pottschach in Lower Austria, near the Styrian border. There the family stayed for the next six years before moving again, this time to Neudörfl on the Hungarian border, in the Burgenland. In such places, then, Rudolf Steiner grew to adolescence, connected to the modern world by the railroad and telegraph but still within the immemorial natural beauty of the Central European landscape. A gifted student, he entered the *Oberrealschule*—the "modern" school in contrast to the "classic" *Gymnasium*— at the tender age of eleven. Thence, in 1879, he went on to the *Technische Hochschule* in Vienna to study natural history, mathematics, chemistry.

There is of course much more to the story—to discover it, interested readers should turn first to the *Autobiography* and then to other accounts.[1] In the texts presented here, we are interested in what shaped Rudolf Steiner as an educator. Certainly, his native clairvoyant capacities played a role, as did his scientific training. Nor should mention be omitted of the crucial human and spiritual encounters that marked his early years: Felix Kogutsky, the herb gatherer, with whom Steiner became friends and with whom he could speak about the spiritual world as with someone of experience;[2] the otherwise unnamed Master;[3] and the various intellectual soul friends and acquaintances—such as Marie Lang and Marie Eugenie della

1. For instance: Stewart C. Easton, *Rudolf Steiner: Herald of a New Epoch*; Rudi Lissau, *Rudolf Steiner: Life, Work, Inner Path, and Social Initiatives*; A. P. Shepherd, *Scientist of the Invisible*; Günther Wachsmuth, *The Life and Work of Rudolf Steiner*; Robert McDermott, *The Essential Steiner*.
2. In his *Autobiography*, Steiner writes further: "He was a deeply pious man. He was quite uneducated in the usual sense of the word. True, he had read many mystical books, but what he said was quite uninfluenced by his reading. It was the outflow of a soul life which bore a quite elementary, creative wisdom within it. One soon realized that he read books only because he was seeking in others what he already knew." See also Emil Bock, "The Search for Felix the Herbgatherer," *The Golden Blade*, 1961. Felix Kogutsky also appears in Steiner's Mystery Dramas as the character Felix Balde.
3. See "Notes by Rudolf Steiner written for Edouard Schuré in Barr, Alsace, September 1907" in Rudolf Steiner and Marie von Sivers, *Correspondence and Documents 1901–1925*.

Grazie,[4] Rosa Mayreder,[5] Friedrich Eckstein,[6] and Karl Julius Schröer[7]—who likewise played their part in his Vienna years and demonstrate the range of Rudolf Steiner's interests. Mention should be made, too, of the philosophers Robert Zimmermann and Franz Brentano, whose lectures Steiner attended; and of Edward Reitlinger, whose lectures on the mechanical theory of heat and on the history of physics also made a deep impression on him. All were important to Rudolf Steiner's formation.

More directly relevant to his development as an educator, however, were his prolonged engagement with the works— above all, the scientific works—of the great German student of nature, poet, dramatist, and novelist Johann Wolfgang von Goethe and the experiences Steiner gained as a tutor.

Though better known as a literary figure—he is usually named with Dante and Shakespeare as one of the three giants of Western literature—at the end of his life Goethe believed his scientific writings would prove of greater consequence in the world than his poems or dramas.[8] As he himself remarked,

---

4. Marie Lang, together with her husband, Franz Hartmann and Friedrich Eckstein formed a theosophical study group with which Rudolf Steiner came into contact in 1888. Here he would have first encountered theosophical literature, such as A.P. Sinnett's *Esoteric Buddhism*. Marie Eugenie delle Grazie was a poet and dramatist. Rudolf Steiner met her at a Saturday evening circle in the home of Laurence Müllner, the Cistercian.
5. Rosa Mayreder (1858–1938) was a well-known writer, painter, freethinker, and woman's advocate. Rudolf Steiner met her through Marie Lang.
6. Friedrich Eckstein (1861–1939)—"dear Eck"—was a close friend and fellow seeker in Steiner's Vienna days who remained in contact with him until his death. Eckstein brought Steiner into early contact with both mystical, esoteric circles and also with devotees of the "new music"—Wagner and Bruckner.
7. Karl Julius Schröer (1825–1900) was an educator, philologist, and Goethe scholar who become Steiner's "fatherly friend" and sponsor during the 1880s. In 1884, he recommended Steiner for the position of editor and commentator on Goethe's scientific writings to the publisher Joseph Kürschner who wished to include them in his series of volumes on German literature.
8. See Eckermann's *Conversations with Goethe*. See also Douglas Miller, *Goethe's Scientific Writings*.

others had perhaps written as well and as deeply as he had, but he alone among his contemporaries had understood the nature of color. And in fact it is true that probably no one in modern times penetrated nature as deeply as Goethe did. From Goethe, Steiner learned above all two things: he learned how to begin to realize an epistemology—or way of knowing the world[9]—that was firmly rooted in experience and was non-dualistic, participatory, and holistic; and at the same time, he was led to understand the universal function of metamorphosis and the polar/triadic nature of all evolutionary phenomena in all nature, including human nature.

As for tutoring, this afforded the young Rudolf Steiner, as he himself says, the sole possibility of a livelihood, while keeping him from becoming one-sided. He began early, taking on his first pupils at the age of fourteen. He writes that he had many pupils, each needing preparation in a different field, so that he found himself preparing lessons in the most varied fields from mathematics to bookkeeping. As he did so, he recognized the truth of his friend and teacher Schröer's belief in "the necessity of a comprehensive development of human nature."

All of this, however, was but preparation for his engagement by the Specht family with whom he lived from 1884 to 1890. As Steiner writes:

> Destiny brought me a special pedagogical task. I was recommended to a family with four boys. Three of them had only to be given preparatory instruction for the elementary school and later supplementary tuition for the secondary school. But the

---

9. Steiner's involvement with Goethe may be traced in the following works: *Goethean Science* [*Goethes Naturwissenschaftliche Schriften. Sämtliche Einleitungen zur Herausgabe in Kürschners "Deutsche National Literatur"*]; *The Science of Knowing* [*Grundlinien einder Erkenntnistheorie der Goetheschen Weltanschauung* (1886)]; and *Goethe's World View* [*Goethes Weltanschauung*(1897)]. See also John Barnes, ed., *Nature's Open Secret: Rudolf Steiner on Goethe* (forthcoming).

fourth, who was about ten years old, was entrusted to me for his entire education. He was a sorrow to his parents, particularly to his mother. When I came into the family he had hardly acquired the rudiments of reading, writing, and arithmetic. He was considered so abnormal in his physical and mental development that the family doubted that he could be educated at all. His thinking was slow and dull. Even slight mental exertion would cause a headache, lowered vitality, pallor, and there would be alarming emotional behavior.

After I had come to know the child, I felt certain that an education adapted to this particular constitution of soul and body would awaken his sleeping capacities, and I proposed to the parents that they leave the method of education in my hands. The boy's mother met my proposal with confidence, and thus I was able to set myself this special pedagogic task.

I had to find access to a soul that was in a kind of sleeping condition and that had gradually to be brought to master the bodily functions. First, the soul had to be helped to fit, as it were, into the body. I was convinced that the boy had great intellectual capacities, though this was not apparent. And this made my task deeply satisfying. After a short time I succeeded in gaining the child's love. This had an awakening effect on his sleeping soul-faculties, merely through my being with him. I had to devise special methods of teaching him. Even a quarter of an hour over and above the specific length of time allotted to lessons caused danger to his health. The boy could find relation to most subjects only with great difficulty.

This pedagogical task became a rich source of learning for me. The educational methods I had to adopt gave me insight into the way the human soul and spirit are connected with the human body. It became my actual training in physiology and psychology. I came to realize that education and teaching must become an art, based upon true knowledge of the human being. I had to adhere to a carefully planned program. In order to make use of the boy's intellectual capacities to the best advantage in the shortest possible time, and with the least strain on his mental and physical forces, I often had to spend up to two hours preparing the material I taught for half an hour. The sequence of the subjects taught had to be carefully arranged and the day divided into definite periods. I had the satisfaction of seeing the boy catch up with the primary school curriculum in the course of two years, and successfully pass the entrance examination for the Gymnasium. His health also improved considerably. The hydrocephalic condition was rapidly diminishing. I could advise the parents to send the boy to the public school, for I thought it essential that he should grow up with other children. I remained with the family for several more years, devoting myself particularly to this boy, whose successful progress through school depended entirely upon the fact that at home his activities continued in the same spirit in which they had begun. This was the occasion to which I referred earlier, when I continued my study of Greek and Latin,[10] for I had to help this and one other boy in the family with these subjects, since they were required for the curriculum of the Gymnasium. I was grateful that destiny brought me such a vital task. I gained insight into human nature in a living, practical way that would have been hardly possible otherwise. . . .[11]

Otto Specht, the young man in question, went on to become a medical doctor, a dermatologist. He died in the First World War, as a result of an infection. For Rudolf Steiner, as he himself says, the experience—when seen in the context of his other intellectual and spiritual activities—was of inestimable value. Through it, he came to understand the complex interplay of body, soul, and spirit in the developmental process that is education. In other words, the pedagogical seed that would germinate thirty years later as Waldorf education was already planted and being watered.

---

10. This was very fortunate, as Paul Allen points out in his edition of the *Autobiography*, because Steiner required Greek and Latin when he took his Ph.D at the University of Rostock.
11. *Autobiography*, Chapter VI.

* * *

STEINER then spent the next decade (more or less) in Weimar, working mostly in the Goethe-Schiller Archives (where he contributed to the famous Weimar edition of Goethe's works). There, one day, he met Elisabeth Förster-Nietzsche, the philosopher's sister, who was just then founding the Nietzsche Archive. As a result, he was able to visit the dying philosopher, spend several weeks in the Nietzsche Archive in Naumberg, and help organize Nietzsche's library. As he writes: "It was a wonderful task to arrange the books Nietzsche had studied. One felt his spiritual presence among his books. A volume of Emerson was filled with marginal comments and showed every sign of devoted study. And so did the writings of Guyau. There were books with passionate criticisms in the margins. In a number of these comments one could detect the germ of many of Nietzsche's ideas."[12]

Such was his outward life at this time: an independent man of letters, a philosopher, scientist, and literary scholar. He received his doctorate from Rostock University in 1891.[13] He worked deeply and passionately on developing an epistemology in harmony with Goethe's scientific method, realizing that in it lay the seeds for the overcoming of the dominant Kantian view. This view restricted human knowing to narrow bounds that excluded whole areas of natural, cosmic, and spiritual existence that he recognized, from experience, were necessary for a complete understanding of humanity's place and participation in true reality.[14] Inwardly, during this period, Steiner strove to unite in an

---

12. See *Autobiography*, Chapter XVIII. Also, Steiner's 1895 work, *Friedrich Nietzsche: Fighter for freedom.*
13. His dissertation is available as *Truth and Knowledge* (Blauvelt, NY: Steinerbooks, 1981).
14. See, above all, *Truth and Knowledge* and *Intuitive Thinking as a Spiritual Path: A Philosophy of Freedom.*

integral modern epistemological form knowledge of the spiritual worlds with knowledge derived through the senses.

Though he managed to accomplish this almost impossible task, this must have been a time of intense inner struggle for Rudolf Steiner. Whatever darkness he endured, however, he saw the first rays of dawn before the century ended. He writes in the *Autobiography*: "During [this] period, when my statements about Christianity seemingly contradict my later ones,[15] a conscious knowledge of true Christianity began to dawn within me. Around the turn of the century this knowledge grew deeper.... This experience culminated in my standing in the spiritual presence of the Mystery of Golgotha in a most profound and solemn festival of knowledge."[16]

Thus fortified, Rudolf Steiner moved to Berlin, where he entered much more directly onto the stage of history. He edited the *Magazin für Literatur*, taught at the Working Men's College (founded by Wilhelm Liebknecht), the Giordano Bruno Union, and began to speak openly of spiritual matters under the auspices of the Theosophical Society—the Secretary of whose German Section he became, on the strict understanding that he would be completely independent and teach only what he wanted. Steiner's independence, in fact, was radical. Entering the stream of the renewal of the ancient Mysteries inaugurated by H.P. Blavatsky—which broke down the barriers between "esoteric" and "exoteric" and undid the separation that had arisen between science, art, and religion—Steiner undertook to speak of nothing that he had not himself experienced. Thus, whatever echoes of theosophical literature and teaching may be found in Steiner's work, these ideas are transformed

---

15. Steiner is referring here to such radical philosophical statements as his *Individualism in Philosophy*.
16. *Autobiography*, Chapter XXVI.

and made authentic in the crucible of his own soul. Nevertheless, theosophy—which he soon began to call "spiritual science," *Geisteswissenschaft*—was the immediate context in and out of which Rudolf Steiner first spoke as an educator.[17]

* * *

THE TEXTS in this volume date from 1906 to 1912 and therefore predate by a number of years the actual founding of the first Waldorf school in 1919. Many of the principles of Waldorf educational theory and practice, however, will be found to be present. The emphasis, of course, is slightly different, for there are not yet actual schools where the vital principles Rudolf Steiner describes may be put into practice. Yet already Steiner is very clear: schools must arise through which the truths of spiritual science may be practically embodied for the benefit of human beings and the ongoing evolution of humanity:

> Spiritual science, by its inherent character and tendency, has the task of providing a practical concept of the world—one that comprehends the nature and essence of human life.... For spiritual science is not intended as a theory that is remote from life, one that merely caters to human curiosity or the thirst for knowledge. Nor is it intended as an instrument for a few people who for selfish reasons would like to attain a higher development for themselves. No, it can join and work at the most important tasks of modern people and further their development for the welfare of humankind.[18]

---

17. Rudolf Steiner continued to teach spiritual science under the auspices of the Theosophical Society until 1912/13. At this time, the break between Rudolf Steiner and Annie Besant and the Adyar theosophists was complete. On February 3, 1913, the first General Meeting of the Anthroposophical Society took place. From then on, Rudolf Steiner worked, researched, and taught within the Anthroposophical Movement. However, this "change" did not alter one iota what he stood for. Therefore, with hindsight and yet in a real sense, one may say that Rudolf Steiner, even as a "theosophist," already taught anthroposophy.

18. From "The Education of the Child," this volume, page 3.

In other words, if the spiritual renewal promised by theosophy was not to be a dead thing, its spiritual science "must provide the most fruitful and practical means for the solution of the urgent questions of modern life." One such question is, of course, education. Steiner is quite clear, however, that whatever guidance spiritual scientific insight can provide to the furtherance of education, this must not take the form of an abstract program but must arise naturally out of the nature of the child, the evolving human being, which contains in itself the seeds of its own future.

Thus these lectures are largely descriptive. In them, Rudolf Steiner describes the picture of the human being as a fourfold being—physical body, life-body or etheric body, sentient or astral body, and the I—showing how these members work together in the evolving human being, as well as in humanity as such. Any educator who recognizes this interaction in the developing child in the classroom will teach differently and will teach different subjects, depending upon the child's age and situation. "The Education of the Child in the Light of Spiritual Science," the first, longest, best-known, and most loved piece in this book, lays out the implications of this view in a masterly way. Originally given as a public lecture in the *Architektenhaus* in Berlin on January 10, 1907—the founding lecture of anthroposophical pedagogy—it appeared in written form in the journal *Lucifer-Gnosis* in April of that year.

The other lectures, while allowing readers to come to know Rudolf Steiner better, amplify and extend the ideas contained in "The Education of the Child." These lectures reveal Steiner's selfless love for human beings, his idealism, and his practicality, and at the same time provide sustenance, inspiration, and many useful insights for teachers and parents alike.

PART ONE

The Education of the Child in the Light of Spiritual Science

Translated by George & Mary Adams

Humankind has inherited much from past generations that is called into question by life today. Hence the numerous "problems of the hour" and "demands of the age." How many of these occupy the attention of the world: social issues, women's issues, various educational questions, questions of health, questions of human rights, and so on? In the most varied ways, human beings are endeavoring to come to terms with these problems. One cannot count the number of people who appear with one or another remedy or program, for the solution—or at least a partial solution—of one or another of them. In the process, all kinds of opinions and shades of opinion assert themselves: radicalism, which carries itself with a revolutionary air; moderate attitudes, full of respect for what exists, yet endeavoring to evolve something new out of it; and conservatism, which is up in arms whenever any of the old institutions are tampered with. Aside from these main tendencies of thought and feeling there is every kind of intermediate position.

Looking at these things in life with deeper vision one can only feel—indeed the impression forces itself upon one—that people of our age are in the position of trying to meet the demands involved in modern life with methods that are utterly inadequate. Many are attempting to reform life without really knowing the foundations of life. But those who would make proposals for the future must not be content with a knowledge of life that only touches life's surface. They must investigate its depths.

Life in its wholeness is like a plant. The plant contains not only what it offers to external life, but it also holds a future state within its hidden depths. One who views a plant just leafing knows very well that after awhile there will be flowers and fruit also on the leaf-bearing stem. The plant already contains in its hidden depths the flowers and fruit in embryo; yet by simply investigating what the plant now offers to external vision, how could one ever tell what those new organs will look like? This can only be told by one who has learned to know the very nature and being of the plant.

Likewise the whole of human life also contains within it the seeds of its own future, but if we are to tell anything about this future, we must first penetrate into the hidden nature of the human being; and our age is little inclined to do this. It concerns itself with the things that appear on the surface, and thinks it is treading on unsafe ground if called on to penetrate what escapes external observation.

In the case of the plant the matter is definitely simpler; we know that others of its kind have previously borne fruit again and again. Human life is present only once; the flowers it will bear in the future have not yet been there. Yet they are present within a human being in the embryo, even as the flowers are present in a plant that is still only in leaf. And there is a possibility of saying something of humankind's future, if once we penetrate beneath the surface of human nature to its real essence and being. The various ideas of reform current in the present age can become fruitful and practical only when fertilized by this deep penetration into human life.

Spiritual science, by its inherent character and tendency, has the task of providing a practical concept of the world—one that comprehends the nature and essence of human life. Whether what often passes as such is justified is not the point; what concerns us here is the true essence of spiritual science, and what it can be by virtue of its true essence. For spiritual science is not intended as a theory that is remote from life, one that merely caters to human curiosity or thirst for knowledge. Nor is it intended as an instrument for a few people who for selfish reasons would like to attain a higher level of development for themselves. No, it can join and work at the most important tasks of modern people and further their development for the welfare of humankind.[1]

It is true that in taking on this mission, spiritual science must be prepared to face all kinds of skepticism and opposition. Radicals, moderates, and conservatives in every sphere of life are bound to meet it with skepticism, because in its beginnings it will scarcely be in a position to please any party. Its promises are far beyond the sphere of party movements—being founded, in effect, purely and solely on a true knowledge and perception of life. If people have knowledge of life, it

---

1. It should not be inferred that spiritual science is only concerned with the greater questions of life. Spiritual science, as expressed here, is destined to provide a basis for the solution of the greater questions of humankind. At the same time it is no less true that spiritual science can bring help to every individual person wherever they find themselves in life; it can be a source from which we may draw the answers to the most common questions, from which we may draw comfort, strength, confidence for life, and work. Spiritual science can give strength for meeting the great life problems, and just as surely also for meeting the immediate needs of the moment, even in the apparently least significant matters of daily life.

is only out of life itself that they can take up their tasks. They will not draw up programs arbitrarily, for they will know that the only fundamental laws of life that can prevail in the future are those that prevail already in the present. The spiritual investigator will therefore of necessity respect what exists. No matter how great the need they may find for improvement, they will not fail to see the embryo of the future within what already exists. At the same time they know that in everything "becoming" there must be growth and evolution. Thus they will perceive the seeds of transformation and of growth in the present. They will invent no programs, but read them from what is already there. What they read becomes in a certain sense the program itself, for it bears within it the essence of development. For this very reason a spiritual-scientific insight into the being of humankind must provide the most fruitful and the most practical means for the solution of the urgent questions of modern life.

In the following pages we shall endeavor to prove this in relation to one particular question: the question of education. We shall not set up demands nor programs, but simply describe child-nature. From the nature of the growing and evolving human being, the proper viewpoint for Education will, as it were, result spontaneously.

. . . .

If we want to perceive the nature of the evolving human being, we must begin by considering hidden human nature as such. What sense observation learns to know in human beings, and what the materialistic concept of life would consider as the only element in human beings, is for spiritual investigation only one part, one member of human nature: that is, the physical body. This human physical body is subject to the same laws of physical existence and is built up of the same substances and forces as the world as a whole, which is commonly referred to as lifeless. Spiritual science, therefore, designates that humankind has a physical body in common with all of the mineral kingdom. And it designates as the *physical body* only what, in human beings, are those substances that mix, combine, form, and dissolve through the same laws that also work in the substances within the mineral world.

Now beyond the physical body spiritual science recognizes a second essential principle in the human being. It is the *life-body*, or *etheric body*. The physicist need not take offense at the term *etheric body*. The word *ether* in this connection does not mean the same as the hypothetical ether of physics.[2] It must simply be taken as a designation for what will be described here and now. Recently it was considered highly unscientific to speak of such an etheric body, although this was not the situation at the end of the eighteenth and during the first half of the nineteenth century. In that earlier time people would say to themselves, "The substances and forces at work in a mineral cannot, by themselves, form the mineral into a living creature. There must also be a peculiar "force" inherent in the living creature. They called this the *vital force* and thought of it somewhat as follows: the vital force works in the plant, the animal, and the human body, and produces the phenomena of life, just as magnetic force is present in the magnet that produces the phenomena of attraction. In the succeeding period of materialism, this idea was dispensed with. People began to say that living creatures are built up in the same way as lifeless creation; that the same forces are at work in both the living organism and in the mineral; that the same forces

---

2. *Ether* was at that time hypothesized by physicists to occupy all of space beyond our atmosphere, and was thought to account for the source of electromagnetic radiation throughout space. — ED.

merely work in a more complicated way and build a more complex structure.

Today, however, it is only the most rigid materialists who hold on to this denial of a life-force, or vital force. There are a number of natural scientists and thinkers who have been taught by facts of life to assume the existence of something like a vital force or life-principle. Thus modern science in its later developments is in a certain sense approaching what spiritual science says about the life-body. There is, however, a very important difference. From sense-perceptible facts modern science assumes, through intellectual considerations or inflections, a kind of vital force. This is not the method of genuine spiritual investigation that spiritual science adopts and on the results of which it bases its statements. It cannot be emphasized too often how great the difference is in this respect between spiritual science and today's modern science. For modern science considers sense experiences to be the foundation for all knowledge. Anything that cannot be built on this foundation is taken to be unknowable. From the impressions of the senses it draws deductions and conclusions. What goes on beyond them is rejected as lying "beyond the frontiers of human knowledge."

From the standpoint of spiritual science, such a view is like that of a blind person who only acknowledges as valid what can be touched and the conclusions deduced from the world of touch—a blind person who rejects the statements of seeing people as lying beyond the possibility of human knowledge. Spiritual science shows that human beings are capable of evolution, capable of bringing new worlds within their sphere by developing new organs of perception. Color and light are all around those who are blind. If they cannot see these things it is simply because they lack the proper organs of perception. Similarly, spiritual science asserts that there are many worlds around human beings who can perceive them only if they develop the necessary organs. Just as a blind person who has undergone a successful operation looks out at a new world, so through the development of higher organs human beings can come to know new worlds—worlds totally different from what our ordinary senses allow us to perceive.

Now whether one who is blind in body can be operated on or not depends on the constitution of the organs. But the higher organs whereby one can penetrate into the higher worlds are present in the embryo of every human being. Anyone can develop these organs who has the patience, endurance, and energy to apply the methods described in *How to Know Higher Worlds: A Modern Path of Initiation.*[3]

Spiritual science, therefore, would never say that there are definite frontiers to human knowledge. What it would rather say is that for human beings those worlds exist for which they have the organs of perception. Thus spiritual science speaks only of the methods whereby existing frontiers may be extended; and this is its position in terms of the investigation of the life-body or etheric body, and of everything specified in the following pages as still higher members of human nature. Spiritual science acknowledges that only the physical body is accessible to investigation using the bodily senses; and, from the perspective of this kind of investigation it would be possible, at most, by intellectual deductions to surmise the existence of a higher body. At the same time it tells how it is possible to open up a world where these higher members of human nature emerge for the observer, just as the color and the light of things emerge after an operation in the case of a person born blind. For those who have developed the higher organs of perception, the etheric or life-body is an object of perception and not merely an intellectual deduction.

---

3. Anthroposophic Press, Hudson, NY, 1994.

Human beings have this etheric or life-body in common with plants and animals. The life-body works in a formative way on the substances and forces of the physical body and thus brings about the phenomena of growth, reproduction, and inner movement of vital body fluids. It is therefore the builder and shaper of the physical body, its inhabitant and architect. The physical body may even be spoken of as an image or expression of the life-body. In human beings the two are nearly—though by no means totally—equal in form and size. However, in animals, and even more so in the plants, the etheric body is very different in both form and extension from the physical.

The third member of the human body is called the *sentient* or *astral body*. It is the vehicle of pain and pleasure, of impulse, craving, passion, and so on—all of which are absent in a creature that consists of only the physical and etheric bodies. These things may all be included in the term *sentient feeling*, or *sensation*. The plant has no sensation. If in our time some learned people see that plants will respond by movement or some other way to external stimulus and conclude that plants have a certain power of sensation, they only show their ignorance of what sensation is. The point is not whether the creature responds to an external stimulus but whether the stimulus is reflected in an inner process such as pain or pleasure, impulse, desire, and so on. Unless we stick to this criterion, we would be justified in saying that blue litmus-paper has a sensation of certain substances, because it turns red through contact with them.[4]

---

4. It is necessary to stress this point, because in our time there is a great need for clarity on such matters. Many people obscure the distinction between a plant and a sentient being, because they are not clear about the true nature of *sensation*. If a being or thing responds in some way to an external stimulus, it is not therefore justified to say that it has a sensation of the impression. It can only be said to have sensation if it *experiences* the impression in its *inner life*—that is, if there is a kind of inward reflection of the outer stimulus.

Humankind, therefore, has a sentient body in common with the animal kingdom only, and this sentient body is the vehicle of sensation or of sentient life.

We must not make the same mistake as certain theosophical circles and imagine that the etheric and sentient bodies consist simply of substances that are finer than those present in the physical body. That would be a materialistic concept of these higher members of human nature. The etheric body is a *force-form*; it consists of active forces, and not of matter. The astral or sentient body is a figure of inwardly moving, colored, and luminous pictures. The astral body deviates in both size and shape from the physical body. In human beings it presents an elongated ovoid form in which the physical and etheric bodies are embedded. It projects beyond them—a vivid, luminous figure—on every side.[5]

Human beings also possess a fourth member of their being, and this fourth member is shared with no other earthly creature. It is the vehicle of the *human I*, of the *human Ego*. The little word *I*—as used, for example, in the English language—is a name essentially different from any other name. To anyone who ponders rightly on the nature of this name, an approach to the perception of true human nature is opened up immediately. All other names can be applied equally by everyone to what they

---

4. (*continued*) The great advances of the natural sciences in our time—for which a true spiritual investigator has the highest admiration—have nevertheless caused a lack of clarity concerning higher concepts. Some biologists do not know what sensation is and thus ascribe it to a being that has none. What they understand by sensation may well be ascribed even to non-sentient beings. What the spiritual science must understand by sensation is completely different.

5. A distinction must be made between human beings' experience of the sentient body within themselves and the perception of the sentient body by a skilled seer. What is referred to here is what is revealed of the sentient body to a developed spiritual eye.

designate. Everyone can call a table "table," and everyone can call a chair "chair," but this is not true of the name "I." No one can use this name to designate another. Every human being can only call themselves "I"; the name "I" can never reach my ear as a description of myself. In designating oneself as I, one has to name oneself within oneself. Human beings who can say "I" to themselves are a world unto themselves. Those religions founded on spiritual knowledge have always had a feeling for this truth; hence they have said, "With the *I*, the *God*, who in lower creatures reveals himself only externally in the phenomena of the surrounding world, begins to speak internally. The vehicle of this faculty of saying "I," of the *I-faculty*, is the *body of the I*, the fourth member of the human being.[6]

This *body of the I* is the vehicle of the higher soul of humankind. With it human beings are the crown of all earthly creation. Now in human beings today the I is in no way simple in character. We may recognize its nature if we compare human beings at different stages of development. Look at an uneducated savage next to a typical European, or again compare the latter with a person of high ideals. All of them have the faculty to say "I" to themselves; the body of the I is present in them all. But uneducated savages, with their I, follow more the passions, impulses, and cravings. More highly developed people say to themselves, "Certain impulses and desires you may follow," while others are held in check or suppressed altogether. Idealists have developed new impulses and new desires in addition to those originally present. All of this has taken place

---

6. The reader must not take offence at the expression "Body of the I." It is certainly not used in any grossly material sense. But in anthroposophical science there is no other possibility than to use the words of ordinary language; and as these are ordinarily applied to material things, they must, in their application to a spiritual science, first be translated into the spiritual.

through the I working upon the other members of the human being. Indeed, this constitutes the special task of the I. Working outward from itself it has to ennoble and purify the other members of human nature.

In human beings who have reached beyond the condition where the external world first placed them, the lower members have changed to a greater or lesser degree under the influence of the I. When human beings are only beginning to rise above the animal, when their I is only just kindled, they are still like an animal insofar as the lower members of their being are concerned. The etheric or life-body is simply the vehicle of the formative forces of life, the forces of growth and reproduction. The sentient body gives expression only to those impulses, desires, and passions, which are stimulated by external nature. As human beings work their way up from this stage of development through successive lives or incarnations to higher and higher evolution, the I works upon the other members and transforms them. In this way the sentient body becomes the vehicle of purified sensations of pleasure and pain, refined wants and desires. And the etheric or life-body also becomes transformed. It becomes the vehicle of habits, of human beings' more permanent intent or tendency in life, of the temperament and memory. One whose I has not yet worked upon the life-body has no memory of experiences in life. One just lives out what has been implanted by Nature.

This is what the growth and development of civilization means for humanity. It is a continual working of the I on the lower members of human nature; this work penetrates all the way into the physical body. Under the influence of the I the whole appearance and physiognomy, the gestures and movements of the physical body, are altered. It is possible, moreover, to distinguish how the different ways of culture or civilization work on the various members of human nature. The ordinary factors of civilization work on the sentient body and permeate it with pleasures and pains, and with impulses and cravings that are different from what it had originally. Again, when a human being is absorbed in the contemplation of a great work of art the etheric body is being influenced. Through the work of art one divines something higher and more noble than is offered by the ordinary environment of the senses, and in this process one is forming and transforming the life-body. Religion is a powerful way to purify and ennoble the etheric body. Here is where the religious impulses have their tremendous purpose in human evolution.

What we call *conscience* is no more than the result of the I's work on the life-body through many incarnations. When people begin to perceive that they should not do one thing or another and when this perception makes a strong enough impression that the impression passes into the etheric body, conscience arises.

Now this work of the I on the lower members may be something that is either proper to the whole human race, or it may be entirely individual—an achievement of the individual I working on itself alone. In the former case the whole human race collaborates, as it were, in the transformation of the human being. The latter kind of transformation depends on the activity of the individual I alone, in and of itself. The I may become so strong that it transforms, through its very own power and strength, the sentient body. What the I then makes of the sentient or astral body is called *spirit-self* (or by the East-ern term, *manas*). This transformation is performed mainly through a process of learning, an enriching of one's inner life with higher ideas and perceptions.

The I can rise to an even higher task, one that belongs essentially to its own nature. This happens not only when the astral body is enriched but also when the etheric or life-body is transformed. People learn many things in the course of life, and if from some point we look back on our past, we can say to ourselves that we have learned much. But we can speak to a far less degree of a transformation in temperament or character during life, or of an improvement or deterioration in memory. Learning relates to the astral body, whereas the latter kinds of transformation relate to the etheric or life-body. It is thus not a happy image if we compare the astral body's degree of change during life with the progress of a clock's minute hand, and the transformation of the life-body with the hour hand's progress.

When people enter into a higher training—or *occult training*, as it is called—above all, it is important to take up this latter formation out of the I's very own power. Individually and with full consciousness, we have to work out the transformation of habits and temperament, character and memory; insofar as we work thus into the life-body, we transform it into what is called in spiritual-scientific terms, *life-spirit* (or, in the Eastern expression, *buddhi*).

At a still higher stage we come to acquire forces whereby we can work upon the physical body and transform it—transforming, for example, the circulation of the blood, the pulse. The amount of the physical body that is thus transformed becomes *spirit-body* (or, in the Eastern term, *atman*).

As a member of the whole human race or some section of it—for example, of a nation, tribe, or family—human beings also attain certain transformations of the lower parts of their nature. In spiritual science the results of this kind of transformation are known as the following: the astral or sentient body, transformed through the I, is called the *sentient soul*; the transformed etheric body is called the *intellectual soul*; and the transformed physical body the *spiritual soul*. We must not imagine that the transformations of these three members take place one after another in time. From the moment the I lights up, all three bodies undergo transformation simultaneously. Indeed, the work of the I does not become clearly perceptible to a person until a part of the spiritual soul has already been formed and developed.

. . . .

From what has been said, it is clear that we may speak of four members of human nature: the *physical body,* the *etheric* or *life-body,* the *astral* or *sentient body,* and the *I-body.* The sentient soul, the intellectual soul, the spiritual soul, and beyond these the even higher members of human nature—spirit-self, life-self, spirit-human being—appear in connection with these four members as products of transformation. When speaking of the vehicles of human qualities, it is indeed only the first four members that are considered.

The educator works on these four members of the human being. Therefore, if we want to work in the right way we must investigate the nature of these parts of human beings. One must not imagine that they develop uniformly in human beings, so that at any given point in life—the moment of birth, for example—they are all equally developed; this is not the situation. Their development occurs differently in the different ages of a person's life. The correct foundation for education and for teaching involves a knowledge of these laws of development of human nature.

Before physical birth, growing human beings are surrounded by the physical body of another. They do not come into independent contact with the physical world. Their environment is the physical body of the mother, and it alone works on them as they grow and ripen. Indeed, physical birth consists in this: the physical mother-body, which has been as a protecting sheath, frees human beings, thus allowing the environment of the physical world to work thereafter directly on them. Their senses open to the external world, and in this way the external world gains an influence over human beings that was previously exercised by the physical envelope of the mother-body.

A spiritual understanding of the world, as represented by spiritual science, sees the birth of the physical body in this process, but not yet that of the etheric or life-body. Even as human beings are surrounded by the physical envelope of the mother-body until the moment of birth, so until the time of the change of teeth—until approximately the seventh year—they are surrounded by etheric and astral envelopes. It is only during the change of teeth that the etheric envelope liberates the etheric body. And an astral envelope remains until puberty when the astral or sentient body also becomes free on all sides, even as the physical body becomes free at physical birth and the etheric body at the change of teeth.[7]

---

7. To object that the child has memory and so on before the change of teeth, or that a child has the faculties connected with the astral body before puberty would indicate a misunderstanding of what is being said here. We must clearly understand that the etheric and astral bodies are present from the beginning, but that they are within their protecting envelopes. It is indeed the protecting envelope that allows the etheric body, for example, to evolve and manifest the qualities of memory very obviously before the change of teeth. But the physical eyes are also present before birth within the protecting envelope of the mother's womb. The eyes are protected in the embryo, and external physical sunlight must not be allowed to affect their development. In exactly the same sense external education must not endeavor to train or influence the shaping of memory before the change of teeth. If, however, we simply nourish it and do not try as yet to develop it externally, we will come to see how memory unfolds during this period, freely and on its own.

It is the same with the qualities that the astral body bears. Before the age of puberty one must nourish them while remembering that the astral body, as explained above, still lies within a protecting envelope. It is one thing to nurture the seeds of development inherent in the astral body before puberty; it is another thing to expose after puberty the now independent astral body to influences in the outer world that it can receive and work on, unprotected by the surrounding envelope. The distinction is certainly a subtle one; but without penetrating it one cannot understand what education truly is.

Thus, spiritual science speaks of three births of human beings. Until the change of teeth certain impressions intended for the etheric body can no more reach it than the air and the struggle of the physical world can reach the physical body while it rests in the mother's womb.

Before the change of teeth occurs, the free life-body is not yet at work in human beings. Just as within the body of the mother the physical body receives forces not its own, gradually developing its own forces within the protecting sheath of the mother's womb, so also are the forces of growth until the change of teeth. During this first period the etheric body is only developing and shaping its own forces together with those—not its own—it has inherited. While the etheric body is thus working its way toward freedom, the physical body is already independent. The etheric body, as it liberates itself, develops and works out what it has to give to the physical body. The second teeth—that is, the person's own teeth—that take the place of those inherited, represent the culmination of this work. They are denser than anything else embedded in the physical body and thus appear last at the end of this period.

After this point the growth of the human physical body is brought about by one's own etheric body alone. But this etheric body is still under the influence of an astral body that has not yet escaped its protecting sheath. At the moment the astral body also becomes free, the etheric body concludes another period of its development; this conclusion is expressed in puberty. The organs of reproduction become independent because, from this time on, the astral body is free, no longer working inwardly, but openly and without its envelope, meeting the external world.

Just as the physical influences of the external world cannot influence the unborn child, so until the change of teeth one should not influence the etheric body with forces that are, for it, the same as the impressions of the physical environment are for the physical body. And in the astral body the corresponding influences should not be allowed influence until after puberty.

Vague and general phrases like "the harmonious development of all the powers and talents in the child," and so on, cannot provide the basis for a genuine art of education. A genuine art of education can only be built on true knowledge of human beings. Not that these phrases are incorrect, but basically they are as useless as saying about a machine that all its parts must be activated harmoniously. To work a machine you must approach it not with phrases and truisms but with real and detailed knowledge. Thus, what is important for the art of education is a knowledge of the members of the human being and of their various developments. We must know what part of the human being especially needs to be worked on at a certain age and how to work on it in the proper way. There is, of course, no doubt that a truly realistic art of education, such as that indicated here, will make its way slowly. This is, indeed, because of the whole mentality of our age, which will continue for a long time to consider facts of the spiritual world to be the empty talk of a wild imagination, while it takes vague and completely unreal phrases as the result of realistic thinking. Here, however, we shall describe unreservedly what will eventually come to be common knowledge, though many today might still consider it a figment of the imagination.

With physical birth the physical human body is exposed to the physical environment of the external world. Before birth it was surrounded by the protecting envelope of the mother's body. What the forces and fluids of the enveloping mother-body have done for it thus far, must from now on be done by the forces and benevolence of the external physical world. Before the change of teeth in the seventh year the human body has to accomplish a task on itself that is essentially different from the tasks of any other period of life. In this period the physical organs must form themselves into definite shapes; their whole structural nature must receive particular tendencies and directions. Growth takes place in later periods as well; but throughout the whole succeeding life growth is based on the forces developed in this first life-period. If true forms were developed, true forces would grow; if misshapen forms were developed, misshapen forms would grow. We can never repair what we have neglected as educators in the first seven years; just as nature causes the proper environment for the physical human body before birth, so after birth the educator must provide for the proper physical environment. The right physical environment alone works on the child in such a way that the physical organs correctly shape themselves.

Two "magic" words indicate how children enter into relationship with their environment. These words are *imitation* and *example*. The Greek philosopher Aristotle called human beings the most imitative of creatures. For no age in life is this truer than for the first stage of childhood, before the change of teeth. Children imitate what happens in their physical environment, and in this process of imitation their physical organs are cast in the forms that thus become permanent. "Physical environment" must, however, be understood in the widest sense imaginable. It includes not just what happens around children in the material sense, but everything that occurs in their environment—everything that can be perceived by their senses, that can work on the inner powers of children from the surrounding physical space. This incudes all moral or immoral actions, all wise or foolish actions that children see.

It is not moralistic talk or wise admonitions that influence children in this sense, but it is, rather, what adults do visibly before their eyes. The effect of admonition is that it shapes the forms—not of the physical, but of the etheric body; and the etheric body, as we saw, is surrounded until the seventh year by a protecting etheric envelope, even as the physical body is surrounded before physical birth by the physical envelope of the mother-body. Everything that must evolve in the etheric body before the seventh year—ideas, habits, memory, and so on—all of this must develop "by itself," just as the eyes and ears develop within the mother-body without the influence of external light. The things that we read in Jean Paul's excellent educational work, *Levana* or *Science of Education,* is no doubt true. He says that travelers have learned more from their nurses in their first years of life than they will in all of their journeys around the world. Children, however, do not learn by instruction or admonition, but through imitation. The physical organs shape themselves through the influence of the physical environment. Good sight will be developed in children if their environment has the proper conditions of light and color, while in the brain and blood circulation the physical foundations will be laid for a healthy moral sense if children see moral actions in their environment. If before their seventh year children see only foolish actions in their surroundings, the brain will assume the forms that adapt it to foolishness in later life.

As the muscles of the hand grow firm and strong through doing the work for which they are suited, so the brain and other organs of the physical body of human beings are guided into the correct course of development if they receive the proper impressions from their environment. An example will best illustrate this point. You can make a doll for a child by folding up an old napkin, making two corners into legs, the other two corners into arms, a knot for the head, and painting eyes, nose and mouth with blots of ink. Or you can buy the child what is called a "pretty" doll, with real hair and painted cheeks. We need not dwell on the fact that the "pretty" doll is of course hideous and apt to spoil the healthy aesthetic sense for a lifetime; for education, the main question is different. If the children have the folded napkin before them, they have to fill in from their own imagination what is necessary to make it real and human. This work of the imagination shapes and builds the forms of the brain. The brain unfolds as the muscles of the hand unfold when they do the work they are suited for. By giving the child the so-called "pretty" doll, the brain has nothing more to do. Instead of unfolding, it becomes stunted and dried up. If people could look into the brain as a spiritual investigator can, and see how it builds its forms, they would certainly give their children only the toys that stimulate and enliven its formative activity. Toys with dead mathematical forms alone have a desolating and killing effect on the formative forces of children; on the other hand whatever kindles the imagination of living things works in the proper way. Our materialistic age produces few good toys. It is certainly a healthy toy, for example, that, with movable wooden figures, represents two smiths facing each other and hammering an anvil. These things can still be bought in rural areas. The picture books where the figures can be moved by pulling threads from below are also excellent and allow children themselves to transform a dead picture into a representation of living action. All of this causes a living mobility of the organs, and through such mobility the proper forms of the organs are built up.

Of course, these things can only be touched on here, but in the future, spiritual science will be called on to give the necessary indications in detail, which it is in a position to do. For it is not an empty abstraction, but a body of living facts that can provide guidelines for the conduct of life's realities.

A few more examples may be given. With regard to the environment, "nervous" children, that is, excitable children, should be treated differently from those who are quiet and lethargic. Everything comes into consideration, from the color of the room and the various objects that are generally around the child, to the color of the clothes they wear. One will often do the wrong thing if one does not take guidance from spiritual knowledge, for in many cases the materialistic idea will be the exact reverse of what is proper. Excitable children should be surrounded by and dressed in red or reddish-yellow colors, while lethargic children should be surrounded by blue or bluish-green shades of color. The important thing is the complementary color that is created within the child. In the case of red it is green, and in the case of blue, orange-yellow. This can be seen very easily by looking for awhile at a red or blue surface and then quickly looking at a white surface. The physical organs of the child create this contrary or complementary color, and this is what causes the corresponding organic structures that the child needs. If excitable children have a red color around them, they will inwardly create the opposite, the green; and this activity of creating green has a calming effect. The organs assume a tendency of calmness.

One thing must be thoroughly and fully recognized for this age in a child's life: the physical body creates its own scale of measurement for what is beneficial to it. It does this by properly developing craving and desire. Generally speaking, we may say that the healthy physical body desires what is good for it. In the growing human being, so long as it is the physical body that is important, we should pay the closest attention to what healthy, craving desire and delight require. Pleasure and delight are the forces that most properly enliven and call forth the organs' physical forms.

In this matter it is all too easy to do harm by failing to bring children into the proper physical relationship with their environment. This may happen especially in regard to their instincts for food. Children may be overfed with things that make them lose completely their healthy instinct for food, whereas by giving them the proper nourishment, the instinct can be preserved so that they always want what is wholesome for them under the circumstances, even a glass of water, and this works just as surely with what would do harm. Spiritual science, when called on to build up an art of education, can indicate all these things in detail, even specifying particular forms of food and nourishment. For spiritual science is realistic and not gray theory; it is something for life itself.

The joy of children in and with their environment, must therefore be counted among the forces that build and shape the physical organs. They need teachers that look and act with happiness and, most of all, with honest unaffected love. Such a love that streams, as it were, with warmth through the physical environment of the children may be said to literally "hatch" the forms of the physical organs.

The children who live in such an atmosphere of love and warmth, and who have around them truly good examples to imitate, are living in their proper element. One should thus strictly guard against anything being done in the children's presence that they should not imitate. One should not do anything that one would then have to say to a child, "You should not do that." The strength of children's tendency to imitate can be recognized by observing how they paint and scribble written signs and letters long before they understand them. Indeed, it is good that they paint the letters first by imitation and only later learn to understand their meaning. For imitation belongs to the time when the physical body is developing, while meaning speaks to the etheric, and the etheric body should not be worked on until after the change of teeth, after the outer etheric envelope has fallen away. All learning associated with speech in these years should be especially through imitation. Children will best learn to speak through hearing; no rules or artificial instruction of any kind can be good for this.

It is important to realize the value of children's songs, for example, as a means of education in early childhood. They must make pretty and rhythmical impressions on the senses; the beauty of sound is of greater value than the meaning. The more alive the impression on eye and ear the better. Dancing movements in musical rhythm have a powerful influence in building up the physical organs, and this should also not be undervalued.

. . . .

With the change of teeth, when the etheric body lays aside its outer etheric envelop, the time begins when the etheric body can be worked on through external education. We must be very clear about what works on the etheric body from the outside. The formation and growth of the etheric body means the shaping and developing of inclinations and habits, of the conscience, character, memory, and temperament. The etheric body is worked on through pictures and examples—that is, through a child's carefully guided imagination. Just as before the age of seven we have to give the child the actual physical pattern to copy, so between the time of the change of teeth and puberty we must bring into the child's environment things that have the proper inner meaning and value. Growing children will now take guidance from the inner meaning and value of things. Whatever is filled with deep meaning that works through pictures and allegories is proper for these years. The etheric body will unfold its forces if a well-ordered imagination is allowed to take guidance from the inner meaning it discovers for itself in pictures and allegories—whether seen in real life or communicated to the mind. It is not abstract concepts that work in the right way on the growing etheric body, but rather what is seen and perceived—indeed, not with external senses, but with the mind's eye. Such seeing and perceiving is the proper means of education for these years.

For this reason it is most important that boys and girls should have for their teachers people who can awaken in them, as they observe them, the proper intellectual and moral powers. As *imitation* and *example* were, as it were, the magic words for education in the first years of childhood, for the years of this second period, the magic words are *discipleship* and *authority.* What children see directly in their educators with inner perception must, for them, become authority—not authority compelled by force, but authority that they accept naturally without question. Through this they will build up their conscience, habits, and inclinations. They will bring their temperament along an ordered path. They will look at things of the world through its eyes, as it were. The beautiful words of a poet who said, "Everyone must choose their heroes, in whose footsteps they will tread as they carve out their paths to the heights of Olympus," have special meaning during this time of life. Veneration and reverence are forces whereby the etheric body grows in the right way. If it were not possible during these years to look up to another person with unbounded reverence, one would have to suffer for this loss throughout all of later life. Where reverence is lacking, the living forces of the etheric body are stunted in their growth.

Picture to yourself how an incident such as the following works on the character of children. An eight-year-old boy hears of someone who is truly worthy of honor and respect. Everything he hears about him inspires holy awe in the boy. The day draws near when he will be able to see him for the first time. With trembling hand he lifts the latch of the door, behind which will appear before him, the person he reveres. The beautiful feelings that such an experience calls forth are among the lasting treasures of life. It is the happy person who, not only in the solemn moments of life but continually, can look up to one's teachers and educators as natural and unquestioned authorities.

Beside these living authorities who embody, as it were, intellectual and moral strength for children, there should also be those they can only apprehend with the mind and spirit, who likewise become their authorities. The outstanding people of history, life stories of great men and women—allow these to determine the conscience and the direction of the mind. Abstract moral maxims are not useful yet; they can only begin to have a beneficial influence when, at the age of puberty, the astral body liberates itself from its astral mother-envelope.

Especially in history lessons, teachers should direct their teaching as indicated. When telling all kinds of stories to little children before their change of teeth, our aim cannot be more than to awaken delight, liveliness, and a happy enjoyment of the story. But after the change of teeth we have to remember something else in selecting material for stories—that is, that we are placing before boys and girls pictures of life that will arouse a spirit of emulation in the soul.

It should not be overlooked that bad habits may be overcome completely by pointing to appropriate examples that shock or repel the child. Reprimands give but little help, at best, in the matter of habits and inclinations. If, however, we show the living picture of a person who has given way to a similar bad habit and allow the child to see where such an inclination actually leads, this will work on the young imagination and go a long way toward uprooting the habit. One fact must always be remembered—that abstract ideas do not influence the developing etheric body but rather, living pictures that are seen and comprehended inwardly. The suggestion that has just been made certainly needs to be carried out with great tact so that the effect is not reversed and results in the very opposite of what was intended. When telling stories everything depends on the art of telling. Word-of-mouth narration cannot, therefore, simply be replaced by reading.

In another connection, for the period between the change of teeth and puberty, it is important to present living pictures—or symbols, as it were—to the mind. It is essential that the secrets of nature, the laws of life, be taught to children, not in dry intellectual concepts, but as far as possible in symbols. Parables of the spiritual connections of things should be brought before the souls of children in such a way that behind the parables they divine and feel, rather than understand intellectually, the underlying law in all existence. "Everything passing is but a parable," must be the maxim guiding all of our education during this time. It is of vast importance for children that they receive the secrets of nature in parables before they are brought before their souls as "natural laws" and so on. An example may serve to make this clear. Let us imagine that we want to tell a child of the immortality of the soul, of the coming forth of the soul from the body. The way to do this is to use a comparison—for example, the butterfly coming out of the chrysalis. As the butterfly soars up from the chrysalis, so after death the human soul comes forth from the house of the body. No one can properly understand this fact in intellectual concepts who has not first received it through such a picture. By a parable such as this we speak not just to the intellect but to the feelings of children, to their whole soul. Children who have experienced this will approach the subject with a completely different mood of soul when later it is taught to them in the form of intellectual concepts. It is a very serious matter indeed for anyone who is not first given the ability to approach the problems of existence through feeling. It is therefore essential that educators have at their disposal parables for all the laws of nature and secrets of the world.

Here we have an excellent opportunity to observe the effects that spiritual-scientific knowledge works to affect in life and practice. When teachers come before their children in class, ready with the parables they "made up" out of an intellectual materialistic way of thinking, in general, they will make little impression upon them, for teachers first have to puzzle out the parables for themselves with all their intellectual cleverness. Parables that first have to be condescended to have no convincing effect on those who listen to them. When one speaks in parables and pictures, it is not just what is spoken and shown that works on the hearer, but a fine spiritual stream that passes from the one to the other, from the one who gives to the one who receives. If the one who tells does not have the warm feeling of belief in the parable, no impression will be made on the other. For true effectiveness, it is essential to believe in one's parables as one does in absolute realities. And this can only be so when one's thought is alive with spiritual knowledge. Take, for example, the parable we have been speaking of. True students of spiritual science need not torment themselves to get it out. For them it is reality. In the coming forth of the butterfly from the chrysalis they see at work, on a lower level of being, the very same process that is repeated, on a higher level, at a higher stage of development, when the soul comes forth from the body. They believe in it with all their might; and this belief streams, as it were, unseen from speaker to hearer, carrying conviction. Life flows freely, unhindered, back and forth from teacher to pupil. But for this it is necessary that teachers draw from the full fountain of spiritual knowledge. Their words, everything that comes from them, must have feeling, warmth, and color from a truly spiritual-scientific way of thought.

A wonderful prospect is thus opened throughout the field of education. If it will only let itself be enriched from the well of life that spiritual science contains, education will also be filled with life and understanding. There will no longer be the groping so prevalent now. All art and practice of education that does not continually receive fresh nourishment from roots such as these is dry and dead. The spiritual-scientific knowledge has appropriate parables for all the secrets of the world—pictures taken from the very being of the things, pictures not first made by human beings, but put in place by the forces of the world within things themselves, through the very act of their creation. Therefore this spiritual knowledge must form the living basis for the whole art of education.

A force of soul that has particular value for this period of human development is memory. The development of the memory is connected with the shaping of the etheric body. Since this shaping occurs so that the etheric body becomes liberated between the change of teeth and puberty, so this is also the time for conscious attention from outside toward the growth and cultivation of the memory. If what is due to human beings at this time has been neglected, their memory will always have less value than it would have had otherwise. It is not possible to make up for later what was left undone.

In this connection many mistakes can be made through an intellectual, materialistic way of thinking. An art of education based on such a way of thought easily arrives at a condemnation of what is mastered simply by memory. It will often place itself untiringly and emphatically against the mere memory training, and will employ the subtlest methods to ensure that children commit nothing to memory that they do not intellectually understand. Yes, and after all, how much has really been gained by such intellectual understanding? A materialistic way of thought is so easily led to believe that any further penetration into things beyond intellectual concepts that are, as it were, extracted from them, simply does not exist; only with great difficulty will it fight its way through to the perception that other forces of the soul are at least as necessary as the intellect to comprehend things. It is no mere figure of speech to say that people can understand with their feeling, their sentiment, their inner disposition, as well as with their intellect. Intellectual concepts are only one way we have for understanding things of this world, and only to the materialistic thinker do they appear as the sole means. Of course there are many who do not consider themselves materialists, who nevertheless consider an intellectual conception of things to be the only kind of understanding. Such people perhaps profess an idealistic or even spiritual outlook. But in their souls they relate themselves to it in a materialistic way, for the intellect is in effect the soul's instrument for understanding what is material.

We have already alluded to Jean Paul's excellent book on education; a passage from it relating to this subject of the deeper foundations of the understanding may well be quoted here. Indeed, Jean Paul's book contains many golden words on education, and deserves far more attention than it has received. It is of greater value for the teacher than many of the educational works currently held in highest regard. One passage follows:

Have no fear of going beyond the childish understanding, even in whole sentences. Your expression and the tone of your voice, aided by the child's intuitive eagerness to understand, will light up half the meaning and with it, in the course of time, the other half. With children as with the Chinese and people of refinement, the tone is half the language. Remember, children learn to understand their own language before they ever learn to speak it, just as we do with Greek or any other foreign language. Trust to time and the connections of things to unravel the meaning. A child of five understands the words "yet," "even," "of course," and "just." But now try to explain these—not just to the child, but to the father! In the one word "of" there lurks a little philosopher! If an eight-year-old child with developed speech is understood by a child of three, why do you want to narrow your language to the little one's child-ish prattle? Always speak to a child some years ahead—do not those of genius speak to us centuries ahead in books? Talk to one-year-olds as if they were two, to two-year-olds as if they were six, for the difference in development diminishes in inverse ratio with age. We are far too prone to credit teachers with all that children learn. We should remember that the children whom we have to educate bear half their world within them, all there and ready-taught—that is, the spiritual half, including, for example, the moral and metaphysical ideas. For this very reason, language, equipped as it is with material images alone, cannot give the spiritual archetypes; all it can do is to illumine them. The very brightness and decisiveness of children should give us brightness and decisiveness when we speak to them. We can learn from their speech as well as teach them through our own. Their word-building is bold, yet remarkably accurate! For example, I have heard the follow-ing expressions used by children three or four: "the bar-reler" (for the maker of barrels); "the sky-mouse" (for the bat); "I am the looking-through person" (standing behind a telescope); "I'd like to be a gingerbread eater"; "he joked me down from the chair"; "see how one o'clock it is?"

It's true that our quotation refers to something other than our immediate subject; but what Jean Paul says about speech has its value in the present connection also. Here there is also an understanding that precedes intellectual comprehension. Little children receive the structure of language into the living organ-ism of their souls and, for this process, do not require the laws of language formation in intellectual concepts. Similarly, for the cultivation of the memory, older children must learn much that they cannot master with their intellectual understanding until years later. Those things are afterward best apprehended in concepts that have first been learned simply from memory during this period of life, just as the rules of language are best learned in a language one can already speak. So much talk against "mindless rote learning" is simply materialistic prejudice. Children, for example, only need to learn the essential rules of multiplication in a few given examples, for which no apparatus is necessary— the fingers are much better for the purpose than any apparatus—they are then ready to get to work and memorize the whole multiplication table. Proceeding in this way, we shall be acting with due regard for growing children's nature. However, we shall be offending against their nature if, at the time when the development of the memory is the important thing, we are calling too much on the intellect.

The intellect is a soul-force only born with puberty, and we should not try to influence it in any way externally before this time. Until puberty children should be storing in their memories the treasures of thought on which humankind has pondered; later intellectual understanding may penetrate what has already been well imprinted in memory during the earlier years. *It is necessary for human beings to remember not only what they already understand, but to come to understand what they already know*—that is, what they have acquired by memory in the way the child acquires language. This truth has a wide application. First there must be an assimilation of historical events through the memory, then the apprehension of them in intellectual concepts; first the faithful commitment to memory of geographical facts and then an intellectual understanding of the connections between them. In a certain sense, understanding things through concepts should proceed from the stored-up treasures of the memory. The more children know in memory before they begin to understand through intellectual concepts the better.

There is no need to emphasize the fact that these things applied only to the period of childhood we are concerned with here, and not later. If at some later age in life one has occasion to take up a subject for any reason, then of course the opposite may easily be the correct and most useful way of learning it, though even here much will depend on the mentality of the person. During the time of life we are now concerned with, however, we must not dry up a child's mind and spirit by filling it with intellectual conceptions.

Another result of materialistic thinking may be seen in the lessons that are based too exclusively on sense-perception. At this time in childhood all perception must be spiritual. We should not be satisfied, for example, with presenting a plant, a seed, a flower to children only as it is perceived with the senses. Everything should become a parable of the spiritual. In a grain of corn there is far more than meets the eye. There is a whole new plant invisible within it. Children must comprehend in a living way with their feeling and imagination that something like a seed has more within it than is sense-perceptible. They must divine through feeling the secrets of existence. One cannot object that pure perception of the senses is obscured in this way—on the contrary, by going no further than what the senses observe, we stop short of the whole truth. For full reality consists of the spirit as well as the substance, and there is no less need for faithful and careful observation when bringing all the faculties of the soul into play, than when only the physical faculties are employed. If people could only see, as the spiritual investigator sees, the desolation achieved in soul and body by instruction based on external perception alone, they would never insist on it as strongly as they do. In the highest sense, what good is it that children have been shown all possible varieties of minerals, plants, and animals, and all kinds of physical experiments, if nothing further is connected with teaching these things—that is, to make use of the parables that the world offers to awaken a feeling for the secrets of the spirit?

Certainly a materialistic way of thinking has little use for what has been said here, and spiritual investigators understand this all too well. But they also know that the materialistic way of thought will never produce a truly practical art of education. As practical as it appears to itself, materialistic thinking is impractical when what is needed is to enter into life in a living way. In the face of reality, materialistic thought is fantastic—although, indeed, to a materialistic thinker spiritual-scientific teaching, adhering as they do to the facts of life, can only appear fantastic. There will no doubt be many obstacles yet to overcome before the principles of spiritual science—which are, in fact, born from life itself—can make their way into the art of education. It cannot be otherwise. At the present time the truths of this spiritual science can only seem strange to many people. Nevertheless, if they are indeed true, they will become part of our life and civilization.

. . . .

Teachers can have the tact to meet any occasion that arises only when they have a conscious and clear understanding of how various subjects and methods of education work in the proper way on growing children. They have to know how to treat the various faculties of the soul—thinking, feeling, and willing—so that their development can react on the etheric body, which during this time between the change of teeth and puberty can attain more and more perfect form under external influences.

By a proper application of fundamental educational principles during the first seven years of childhood, the foundation is laid for the development of a strong and healthy *will*; for a strong and healthy will must have its support in well-developed forms of the physical body. Then, from the change of teeth on, the etheric body that is now developing must bring to the physical body the forces whereby it can make its forms firm and inwardly complete. Whatever makes the strongest impression on the etheric body also works most powerfully toward consolidating the physical body. The strongest of all the impulses that can work on the etheric body come from the feelings and thoughts through which human beings consciously divine and experience their relationship to the Eternal Powers—that is, they come from religious experience. Never will a person's will—nor as a result a person's character—develop in a healthy way, if one cannot during this period of childhood receive religious impulses deep into the soul. How people feel their place and part in the universal whole will be expressed in the unity of their life of will. If they do not feel linked with strong bonds to a divine-spiritual, their will and character must remain uncertain, divided, and unsound.

The world of *feeling* is developed in the proper way through parables and pictures, which we have spoken of, and especially through the pictures of great men and women, taken from history and other sources and brought before children. A correspondingly deep study of the secrets and beauties of nature is also important for the proper formation of the world of feeling. Last but not least, there is the cultivation of a sense of beauty and the awakening of the artistic feeling. The musical element must bring to the etheric body the rhythm that will then enable it to sense in everything the rhythm otherwise concealed. Children who are denied the blessing of having their musical sense cultivated during these years will be the poorer because of it for the rest of their lives. If this sense were entirely lacking, whole aspects of the world's existence would necessarily remain hidden, nor should the other arts be neglected. The awakening of the feeling for architectural forms, for molding and sculpting, for line and design, for color harmonies—none of these should be left out of the plan of education. No matter how simple life must be under certain circumstances, the objection can never be valid that the situation does not allow something to be done in this way. Much can be done with the simplest resources, if only the teacher has the proper artistic feeling, joy, and happiness in living, a love of all existence, a power and energy for work—these are among the lifelong results of the proper cultivation of a feeling for beauty and art. The relationship of person to person—how noble, how beautiful it becomes under this influence! Again, the moral sense is also being formed in children during these years through the pictures of life placed before them, through the authorities whom they look up to—this moral sense becomes assured if children, from their own sense of beauty, feel that the good is beautiful, and also that the bad is ugly.

Thought in its proper form, as an inner life lived in abstract concepts, must still remain in the background during this period of childhood. It must develop of itself, as it were, without external influences, while life and the secrets of nature are being unfolded in parable and picture. Thus between the seventh year and puberty, thought must be growing, the faculty of judgment ripening, in among the other experiences of the soul; so that after puberty is reached, young people may be able to form independently their own opinions about the things of life and knowledge. The less direct the influence is on the development of judgment in earlier years, and the more a good indirect influence is exercised through the development of the other faculties of soul, the better it is for all of later life.

Spiritual-scientific insights afford the true foundations, not just for spiritual and mental education, but also for physical education. This can be illustrated by referring to children's games and gymnastic exercises. Just as love and joy should permeate children's surroundings in the earliest years of life, so through physical exercises the growing etheric body should experience an inner feeling of its own growth, of its continually increasing strength. Gymnastic exercises, for example, should be such that each movement, each step, gives rise to the feeling within a child: "I feel growing strength within me." This feeling must take hold in the child as a healthy sense of inner happiness and ease. To think out gymnastic exercises from this perspective requires more than intellectual knowledge of human anatomy and physiology. It requires an intimate intuitive knowledge of the connection between a sense of happiness and an ease of positions and movements of the human body—a knowledge that is not merely intellectual, but permeated with feeling. Those who arrange such exercises must be able to experience in themselves how one movement and position of the limbs produces a happy and easy feeling of strength, while another, as it were, an inner loss of strength. To teach gymnastics and other physical exercises with these things in mind, the teacher will need what only spiritual science—the spiritual-scientific habit of mind—can give. They do not need to see directly into the spiritual worlds themselves, but they must have the understanding to apply in life what springs only from spiritual knowledge. If the knowledge of spiritual science were applied in practical spheres such as education, the idle talk that such knowledge has to be proved first would quickly disappear. Those who apply it correctly will find that the knowledge of spiritual science proves itself in life by making life strong and healthy. They will see it is true because it is valid in life and practice, and in this they will find a proof stronger than all the logical, so-called scientific arguments can afford. Spiritual truths are best recognized in their fruits and not by what is called a proof, no matter how scientific; indeed, such proof can never be more than logical skirmishing.

At the age of puberty the astral body is first born. Henceforth the astral body in its development is open to the outside world. Therefore, now we can approach the child only from the outside, with everything that opens up the world of abstract ideas, the faculty of judgment, and independent thought. It has already been pointed out how, until this time, these faculties of soul should be developing free from outer influence within the environment provided by the education that is proper to the earlier years, even as the eyes and ears develop free from outer influence within the organism of the mother. With puberty the time has arrived when human beings are ripe for the formation of their own judgments about what they have already learned. Nothing is more harmful to children than to awaken independent judgment too early. Human beings are not in a position to judge until they have collected material for judgment and comparison in their inner life. If they form their own conclusions before doing so, their conclusions will lack foundation. Educational mistakes of this kind are the cause of all narrow one-sidedness in life, and all barren creeds based on a few scraps of knowledge, ready on this basis to condemn ideas experienced and proven by humankind often throughout long ages.

One's ripeness for thought requires that one has learned to be full of respect for what others have thought. There is no healthy thought that has not been preceded by a healthy feeling for the truth, a feeling for the truth supported by faith in authorities accepted naturally. If this principle were observed in education there would no longer be as many people who all too quickly imagine themselves ripe for judgment, and spoil their own power to receive openly and without bias the general impressions of life. Every judgment that is not built on a sufficient foundation of gathered knowledge and experience of soul throws a stumbling block in the way of those who form it. For having once pronounced a judgment on a matter, we are thereafter influenced by this judgment. We no longer receive the new experiences we would if we had not already formed a judgment about it. Thought must take hold in a living way in children's minds so that they first learn and then judge. What the intellect has to say about any matter should only be said when all the other faculties of the soul have spoken. Before then the intellect only has an intermediary part to play; its task is to comprehend what occurs and what is experienced in feeling, to receive it exactly as it is, not letting unripened judgment immediately come in and take over. For this reason, until puberty children should be spared all theories about things; the main consideration is that they should simply meet the experiences of life, receiving them into their souls. Certainly they can be told what various people have thought about this and that, but exercises of judgment, too early, about one view or another must be avoided. Thus, children should receive people's opinions with the feeling power of the soul. Without jumping to a conclusion or taking sides with this or that person, they should be able to listen to all, saying to themselves: "So and so said this, and another said that." The cultivation of such a mind in a boy or girl certainly demands the exercise of great tact from teachers and educators; but tact is just what spiritual-scientific thought offers.

All we have been able to do is to unfold a few aspects of education in the light of spiritual science. And this alone was our intention—to indicate how great the task is that the impulse of spiritual-science must fulfill in education for the culture of our time. Its power to fulfill the task will depend on the spread of an understanding for this way of thinking in wider and wider circles. For this to happen, however, two things are necessary.

First, people should relinquish their prejudices against spiritual science. Anyone who honestly pursues it will soon see that it is not the fantastic nonsense that many today consider it to be. We are not making any reproach against those who hold this opinion; for everything that the culture of our time offers tends, on a first acquaintance, to make one consider the adherents of spiritual science to be fantastic dreamers. Superficial consideration can reach no other judgment, for in the light of it, spiritual science with its claim to be a science of the spirit will appear to be in direct contradiction to everything that modern culture gives to humankind as the foundation of a healthy view of life. Only a deeper consideration will reveal that the views of the present day are in themselves deeply contradictory and will remain so as long as they are without the spiritual-scientific foundation. Indeed, by their very nature they call out for such a foundation and cannot in the long run exist without it.

The second thing that is needed concerns the healthy cultivation of spiritual science itself. Only when it is perceived in spiritual-scientific circles everywhere that the point is not merely to theorize about the teachings, but to let them bear fruit in the most far-reaching way in all the relationships of life—only then will life itself open up to spiritual science with sympathy and understanding. Otherwise people will continue to consider it a variety of religious sectarianism for a few cranks and enthusiasts. If, however, it performs positive and useful spiritual work, the spiritual science movement cannot in the long run be denied intelligent recognition.

PART TWO

Teaching from a Foundation
of Spiritual Insight

BERLIN, MAY 14, 1906

Translated by Robert F. Lathe & Nancy Parsons Whittaker

I HAVE often repudiated prejudices that foster the idea of theosophy as foreign to practical life. On the contrary, I have often spoken of how theosophy can lead us into practical life, because it teaches the laws that continuously form life around us. If you know only the laws of ordinary life, then you know only a small part of life. The major portion lies in those things hidden in life—that is, hidden from ordinary senses. People will soon recognize that to live better they must study the hidden worlds, since the materialistic approach leads to a crisis in nearly every area, but primarily in health care and education. The question arises of how we should educate people in the coming generations. Materialism leads to a crisis in all important social, political, and cultural questions, since if we followed this path life would eventually be such that we would no longer know how to help ourselves. To illustrate this I would like to say a few things of general interest about the question of education.

Those who consider education in a materialistic way will easily come to distorted conclusions. They will fail to consider the strong regularities of life and will therefore not consider the existence of clearly delineated periods of life. They simply cannot imagine, for example, why the period of childhood ending around age six to eight years is so fundamentally different from the period beginning at approximately age seven and continuing until puberty. If you have no idea of what happens to people during this time, you cannot imagine how important it is to observe it accurately. It is not of little importance to know what people are like during the first three periods of life. The first period proceeds until six to eight years of age, the second until the age of fourteen or fifteen, and the following period includes the next seven to eight years. We need to study these three stages in human life very accurately, not just externally but also from the standpoint of spiritual science, for spiritual science concerns itself with those worlds hidden from the ordinary senses.

You know that the human being does not consist of only the physical body; the human being also consists of an etheric body, which forms the basis of the physical and has a similar shape, and an astral body, which for the clairvoyant appears similar to a cloud, and in which the first two bodies are embedded. Within these, we find the vehicle of the I. We want to look more closely at these three bodies of the developing human being.

If you want to create a complete picture of the human being, then you must recall that a time exists before we can see people physically—that is, the time before birth when the child lives in the mother's body. On a purely physical level, you must differentiate clearly between the period before birth and the following periods, since the child could not live if born too early, if the child were to enter the ordinarily visible world too early. The child could not live because the sense organs, the means of interacting with the outer world, are not yet well enough developed. Those organs—the eyes, ears, and everything needed to live in the physical world—develop during the time before birth while the child is still embraced by the mother's body. The child cannot come into contact with the physical world before its organs develop sufficiently within the protective mantle of another physical body. Birth occurs when a child is mature enough to encounter the physical environment without a protective mantle. We cannot say the same of the etheric and astral bodies. They are not nearly developed to the degree that they could come into direct contact with the physical surroundings.

During the period from birth until about seven years of age, the etheric body undergoes a process similar to that undergone by the physical body before birth. Only at the end of that time can we say that the etheric body is "born." In the same way, the astral body is "born" at the age of fourteen or fifteen, and can then unfold its free and independent activity in the world.

You need to be aware that we may not place any particular demands on the etheric body until the age of seven, nor on the astral body until the age of fourteen. Exposing the baby's etheric body to the brutal demands of the world would be the same as exposing the fetus to the physical world in the fifth month of pregnancy, although we could not see it so readily. The same is true of exposing the astral body before the age of fourteen. Allow me to restate what I have just said. Until the age of seven, only the physical body is developed well enough to withstand the full effects of the world. Until that time, the etheric body is so occupied with its own development that it would be detrimental to try to affect it. Until then, we may, therefore, work only with the physical body. From the age of seven until fourteen, we may take up the development of the etheric body, and only beginning with the age of fifteen can we work upon the astral body.

To affect the human physical body means to provide the child with external stimuli. Such impressions act to develop the physical body, and for this reason, we can hardly compensate for things neglected before the age of seven. Until the age of seven, the physical body exists in a state that requires external sense impressions to develop it. If a child's eye sees only beautiful things until the age of seven, the eye will develop so that it retains a feeling for beauty throughout life. Afterward, the child's sense of beauty can no longer develop in the same way. What you say to a child and what you do until the age of seven are much less important than the environment you create, what the child sees and hears. During this time, we must use external stimuli to support the child's inner growth. The child's free spirit creates a human figure from a piece of wood using only a couple of holes and some marks for the eyes, nose and mouth. If you give a child a beautiful doll, then the child becomes bound to it. The child's inner spirit clings to it and cannot develop its own activity; in this way, children almost entirely lose their imaginative powers.

It is essentially the same with all impressions of the sense-perceptible world. Who you are in the presence of the child, what the child sees or hears, is important. The child will become a good person when surrounded by good people. Children imitate their surroundings. We must place particular value upon learning by example and the child's capacity to imitate. Thus, the correct thing to do is to act so the child can imitate as much as possible. In that sense, we must emphasize the child's physical development between the first and seventh year. During that period we cannot affect the higher bodies through educational methods, quite certainly not through conscious education. You affect these bodies through who you are insofar as they are not occupied with their own development. People can activate the child's good sense through their own good sense. Just as the mother's healthy body has a healthy effect upon the child's body, the teacher must attempt to be a well-rounded and self-contained person, to have high and good thoughts while in the presence of the child.

At the age of seven the period begins when you can deliberately affect the etheric body. Here, two things connected with the development of the etheric body come into consideration—that is to say, habit and memory. The development of the etheric body depends on habits and remembrances. For this reason you should try to give children a firm foundation for life anchored in good habits. People who act differently every day, who lack a stable basis for their deeds, will later lack character. The task to fulfill between the ages of seven and fourteen is to create a basic set of habits and to stimulate memory development. Children need to learn upright habits and to have a rich store of memorized knowledge.

It is an erroneous belief of our materialistic times that very young children should learn to decide for themselves. On the contrary, we should do everything possible to hinder that. During this period of childhood, children should learn through authority. During the second seven-year period, people should instruct children and not teach through example. We form a strong memory, not by explaining all the "whys" and "wherefores," but through authority. We must surround children with people they can count on, people they can trust—people who can awaken in children a belief in the authority they hold. Only after this stage of life should we guide children into their capacity for judgment and independent reason. By freeing the child from the limitations imposed by authority, you rob the etheric body of the possibility of a well-founded development.

During the second seven-year period, it is best to give children examples and analogies, not proofs and conclusions. Conclusions affect the astral body, which is not yet free to receive them. You should tell children about great people, tell them in a way that great historical figures become examples for them. The same is true concerning questions of death and birth. If you can draw examples from nature, you will see what can be accomplished.

You could show children a caterpillar, how it spins a cocoon and afterward a butterfly emerges. This is a wonderful example of how the child is created from the mother. You can accomplish a great deal if you use examples from nature.

It is just as important to teach children moral parables and not moral rules. We can clearly see this in a few sayings from Pythagoras. Instead of saying, "If you want to accomplish something, concern with things that you can see from the start will only be futile," Pythagoras simply said, "Don't strike at fire with your sword." In another example instead of saying, "Don't meddle with things you know nothing about," Pythagoras said, "Keep your bean." Along with the physical meaning, there is also a moral meaning here. In ancient Greece when people needed to make a decision they passed out black and white beans and then counted the number of beans of each color returned. That is how they took votes. In this sense, instead of saying, "Don't meddle in public affairs you know nothing about," Pythagoras said simply, "Keep your bean."

In this way, you can appeal to the formative forces of imagination and not to those of the intellect. The more you use pictures, the more you affect the child. Goethe's mother could not have done anything better for him than to tell moral stories. She never preached at him. Sometimes she did not finish the story, so he made up the ending himself.

If we force children into critical thinking before the age of fourteen, it is particularly disadvantageous for them and forces them to create their own conclusions or lose the well-intended power of the surrounding persons of authority. It is very bad if children cannot look up to anyone. The etheric body becomes stunted, weak, and shallow from lack of good examples on which to build. It is also particularly bad if children prematurely determine their religion and draw conclusions about the world. Children can do this only when their astral bodies can unfold freely. The more we protect children from premature judgmental and critical activities, the better it is for them. When the child's astral body has not yet become free, a wise teacher attempts to make reality comprehensible through the events themselves. Wise teachers do not demand a firm decision about religious confession, as is increasingly the common way of materialistic education.

The chaotic conditions between the religious confessions would quickly dissolve if we adhered to this more often. We should develop the capacity for judgment and reason as late as possible, only after the children's sense of individuality awakens—that is, when the astral body emerges. Before then children should not decide for themselves whom they believe but, instead, that should be a given. In the years that follow, the interrelationships of the sexes most strongly express individuality, that is, when one individual feels drawn to another.

You can see that if you study the three human bodies properly, you will find a practical basis for the proper education of children. Spiritual science is not impractical, not something living in the clouds; rather, spiritual science can provide the best guide for working with life.

That is precisely why we need a deepening of spiritual-scientific insight today, since without it humanity would reach a dead end. People today criticize the past, saying children were not called on at an early enough age to decide about God and the world, but in reality that was a healthy instinct. Now we must achieve that instinctive knowledge more consciously. The instinctive knowledge of earlier times disappeared, and along with it a certain feeling of certainty about life's details. On the other hand, we cannot suddenly damn humanity.[1] If we had strictly followed the dictates of materialism concerning

---

1. The original is unclear at this point.

education, medicine, justice, and so on, then human society would have fallen apart long ago. However, we did not destroy everything, and some of the past still remains alive. We need the spiritual-scientific movement because materialism would, of necessity, lead people to a dead end.

Teachers who still have a feeling for the child's soul suffocate under a school bureaucracy and regulations that are only carica- tures of what should actually exist, and they arise from a super- stitious belief that teachers should deal only with the physical body. This belief exists despite their own religious beliefs.[2] It is important that people gain a sense of the spiritual and what exists beyond sense-perceptible life. Those who cling to educa- tional formulas will never find the right things to do. They cling to traditional church dogmas and don't want to know anything about spiritual development. But we seek spiritual development, since the answers to today's needs must come from the spiritual worlds. The fruits of materialism only cause illness in the human physical and higher bodies. We cannot avoid a major crisis if people do not take up a spiritual deepening.

Many things point clearly to important decisions now being made within our society, but you must look beneath the sur- face—superficial considerations are insufficient. We cannot do away so easily with people's spiritual desires and tendencies. Spiritualism meets the needs of some people who have such desires, but it attempts materialistically to prove spiritual exist- ence. The Catholic Church has a remarkable relationship to spiritualism, given that the Church should be concerned only with spiritual matters, and that every act of the Church should reflect the spirit. A recent event is very curious. A member of the Church sought material proof of the existence of the spirit. A book by Lapponi, the Pope's personal physician, recently

---

2. The original is unclear at this point.

appeared in which he supports spiritualism. This is so remarkable because the book apparently addresses people who are no longer spiritually sensitive; they need clear material proof for the existence of a spiritual world. We certainly have something to think about when the Pope's personal physician openly supports spiritualism. Clearly, he wants to know that the spiritual world exists, but he has no understanding of the Church's teachings about the spiritual world.

In this way, materialism sneaks into religion, into what should not be materialistic at all. You can see from this the importance of a movement such as ours, which appeals to real human understanding of the spirit without asceticism and withdrawal from life, that continually attempts to render the practicality of spiritual life comprehensible.

We should not, however, ask how we can quickly develop occult powers or how we can encapsulate ourselves so that we do not encounter reality. Anyone who asks such questions is only an egoist—no more than a spiritual gourmet. If you want to partake only in what you find spiritually pleasing, then you are only slightly more subtle that someone who begins the day with a gourmet breakfast. Someone with jaded physical taste often creates the tastiest spiritual dishes. In the proper sense, you are a theosophist only if you exert yourself to comprehend and serve life. Parents are theosophically-minded when they see that their task is to support their children at every step on the path of development. Don't ask, "How can we do that these days?" You should know that the important thing is to consciously remember that the soul is eternal.

People readily believe in eternal life, a life they want to begin as quickly as possible after death. For those truly convinced of the eternity of the soul; the period between two and eighty years of age is only seventy-eight years and has but little significance compared to eternity. Such people believe in eternal existence and feel the need for patience. We must become accustomed to acting in the service of all humanity. It is not so important that we immediately use what we learn. Instead, we must continue to try to use it, and eventually we will find some small area of application. We will never achieve this if we merely criticize everything. It is better to do whatever we can and not complain about how little we can use of what we have learned, rather than to do nothing at all. We should accept this in our souls as something truly practical. When we work in that way with spiritual science, our lives will automatically change. Without realizing it, people can change the world when they become theosophists. The main thing is that we gain a true understanding of spiritual science and then to live by it. That is the wise thing to do since it is then applied in life, and the remainder will happen by itself. A mother, a teacher, a theosophist will automatically act differently from one who is not aware. If you know what a human being truly is, then you will instinctively see the changes in the developing child. Most important, however, is that through genuine theosophical insight all the hypocrisy will cease—such as the tomfoolery the "great" people around us practice and transform into seriousness when they address questions of raising children. This happens because people have no faith in the spirit.

Here we have a small insight into spiritual science. It is a part of practical life. We can see that the opponents' claim that it distances us from life is only nonsense; in truth, it leads us into life. Every narrow-minded Tom, Dick, and Harry believe they are above theosophy when they speak about it, but a time will come when they will think differently. In the future such people will be called reactionaries, unable to move into the future—people who did not want to know about practical life or what theosophy could tell us about the spirit. It will be said that they had no desire to learn about practicality from the theosophical convictions living and burning within us.

Education in the Light
of Spiritual Science

COLOGNE, DECEMBER 1, 1906

Translated by Rita Stebbing

W HEN the spiritual-scientific movement began its activity some thirty years ago, its aim was not to satisfy curiosity about the spiritual worlds, but to make spiritual knowledge available to a wider public, and provide insight that will help solve not just spiritual problems but everyday practical problems as well. The subject of today's lecture is one such problem. It is part of everyday life and should be of interest to everyone. Knowledge of human nature and problems of education are intimately connected. No aspect of social life can benefit more from spiritual research than education, because supersensible knowledge can provide practical guidelines in this realm.

To deal with this subject we must again look at the nature of human beings. For spiritual science, that aspect of the human beings understood by the intellect is only part of their nature. The physical, bodily aspect that we can see and touch is what a person has in common with the rest of the natural world. The spiritual investigator's research is not based on speculation, but on what is discovered through the higher sense of clairvoyant sight. This reveals the ether body as the second member of a person's being. It is a spiritual organism, considerably more delicate and refined than the physical body. It has nothing to do with physical ether, and is best described as a sum of forces or currents of energy rather than as substance.

The ether body is the architect of the physical body. The physical body crystallizes out of the ether body much as ice crystallizes out of water. We must therefore regard everything that constitutes the physical aspect of a person's being as having evolved from the ether body. Human beings have this member in common with every being endowed with life—that is, with the vegetable and animal kingdoms. In shape and size the ether body coincides with the physical body except for the lower part, which differs in shape from the physical. The ether body in animals extends far beyond the physical body. For one who has developed the spiritual faculties asleep in every human being, there is nothing fantastic about this description of the ether body—in the same way that it is not fantastic for a person who can see to describe colors such as blue or red to a blind person.

The third member of a person's being, the astral body, bears all kinds of passions—lower as well as higher—joys and sorrows, pleasure and pain, cravings and desires. Our ordinary thoughts and will-impulses are also contained in the astral body. Like the ether body, it becomes visible when the higher senses are developed. The astral body permeates the physical and ether bodies and surrounds humans like a kind of cloud. We have this in common with the animal kingdom. It is in continuous movement, mirroring every shade of feeling. But why the name *astral*?

The physical substances that make up the physical body connect it with the whole Earth; similarly, the astral body is connected with the world of stars. The forces that permeate the astral body and condition a person's destiny and character were called *astral* by those who could look deeply into their mysterious connection with the astral world surrounding the Earth.

The fourth member of a person's being, the power that enables one to say "I," makes the human being the crown of creation. This name can only be applied to oneself; it expresses the fact that the soul's primordial divine spark is what speaks. We share the designations of everything else with others; a person's ear can be reached from outside, but not the name that refers to what is god-like in every individual human soul. That is why in Hebrew esoteric schools it was called the "inexpressible name of God, Jahve," and "I Am the I Am." Even the priest could utter it only with a shudder. The soul ascribes "I am the I am" to itself.

The human physical body is related to the mineral kingdom, the ether body to the vegetable kingdom and the astral body to the animal kingdom. Human beings have the I in common with no other earthly being; the I makes a human being the crown of creation. This fourfold entity has always been known in esoteric schools as the "quaternity of human nature."

These four bodies develop in each person in a particular way, from childhood until old age. That is why, if we are to understand a person, we must always consider each human being individually. A person's characteristics are indicated already in the embryo. However, humans are not isolated beings, but develop within a certain environment and thrive only when surrounded by all the beings of the universe. During embryonic life they must be enveloped by the maternal organism from which they become independent only when a certain stage of maturity is reached. During further development a child goes through more events of a similar nature. Just as the physical body during the embryonic stage must be enveloped by the maternal organism, so is it surrounded after birth by spiritual sheaths related to spiritual realms. The child is enveloped by an etheric and an astral sheath and reposes in them just as the child did in the womb before birth.

At the time of the change of teeth an etheric covering loosens itself from the ether body, as the physical covering did at physical birth. That means that the ether body is born and becomes free in all directions. Until then an entity of like nature to itself was attached to it, and spiritual currents flowed from this entity through it just as physical currents flowed from the maternal covering through the child before birth. Thus, the child is born a second time when the ether body is born. Meanwhile the astral body is still surrounded by its protective sheath—a covering that strengthens and invigorates it until puberty. Then that also withdraws, the birth of the astral body takes place, and the child is born a third time.

The fact that a threefold birth occurs indicates that these three entities must be considered separately. While it is impossible for external light to reach and harm the eyes of the unborn child, it is not impossible—though certainly highly damaging to the soul—that foreign influences can be brought to bear on the ether body before it has become completely independent. The same applies to the astral body before puberty. We should, according to spiritual science, avoid all education and training before the change of teeth, except what relates to the child's physical body; indeed, we should influence the ether body as little as we influence the child's physical body before birth. However, just as the mother must be cared for because her health influences the development of the embryo, so one should now respect the inviolability of the ether body for the benefit of the child's healthy development. This is important because, before the change of teeth, only the physical body is ready for the influences of the external world; all training should be restricted, therefore, to what concerns the physical body. Any external influence of the ether body during this period is a violation of the laws that govern human development.

The human ether body is different from that of the plant world because it becomes, in a person, the bearer of enduring traits such as habits, character, conscience, memory, and temperament. The astral body is the seat of both the life of feelings already mentioned, and the ability to discern, to judge.

These facts indicate the correct time to exert influence on the natural tendencies. In the period until the seventh year the child's bodily faculties develop; they become independent and self-contained. The same applies to the time between the seventh and the fourteenth years concerning habits, memory, temperament, and so on; the time between the fourteenth and the twentieth or twenty-second years is when the faculty of critical intellect develops, and a certain independence of the surrounding world is attained. All these things indicate that different principles of education are required in the various life periods. Special care must be exercised until the seventh year concerning everything that affects the physical body. This includes a great many things. It is a time when all the essential physical organs are gradually developing and the effect on the child's senses is of immense importance. It matters greatly what is seen, heard, and absorbed in general. The faculty most prominent at this time is imitation. The Greek philosopher Aristotle remarked that human beings are the most imitative of all animals. This is especially true of a child before the change of teeth. Everything is imitated during this time, and since whatever enters a child through the senses as light and sound works formatively on the organs, it is most important that what surrounds the child should be beneficial.

At this age nothing is accomplished through admonition; commands and prohibitions have no effect at all. But the *example* is most significant. What children see, what happens in their surroundings, they feel must be imitated. For example, parents were astonished to discover that their well-behaved child had taken money from a cashbox; greatly disturbed, they thought the child was inclined to steal. Questioning revealed that the child had simply imitated what his parents were seen to do every day.

It is important that the examples the child sees and imitates are of a kind that awaken inner forces. Exhortations have no effect, but the way a person acts in the child's presence matters greatly. It is far more important to refrain from doing what the child is not permitted to do than to forbid the child to imitate it.

It is vital, therefore, that during these years educators are exemplary examples, that they only do what is worthy of imitation. Education should consist of example and imitation. The truth of this is recognized when one gains insight into the nature of human beings, and it is confirmed by the results of education based upon it. Therefore, because the capacity to understand what things *mean is* a function of the ether body, the child should not learn the significance of the letters of the alphabet before the change of teeth; before then, children should do no more than trace their form with paint.

Spiritual research makes all these subtleties understandable and sheds light even on the details of what should be done. Everything the child perceives—also in a moral sense—acts on the formation of its physical organs. It does make a difference whether the child is surrounded by pain and sorrow or happiness and joy. Happiness and joy build sound organs and lay the foundation for future health. The opposite can create a disposition toward illness. Everything that surrounds the child should breathe an atmosphere of happiness and joy, including objects, colors of clothing, and wallpaper. The educator must ensure that this is the situation, while also considering the child's particular disposition.

A child who is inclined to be too earnest and too quiet will benefit from being surrounded by rather sombre, bluish, greenish colors, while a lively, over active child should have yellow, reddish colors. This may seem like a contradiction but, in fact, through its inherent nature the sense of sight calls up the opposite colors. The bluish shades have an invigorating effect, while in the lively child the yellow-reddish shades call up the opposite colors.

So you can see that spiritual investigation sheds light even on practical details. The developing organs must be treated in ways that promote their health and inner forces. The child should not be given toys that are too finished and perfect, such as building blocks or perfect dolls. A doll made out of an old table napkin on which eyes, nose and mouth are indicated is far better. Any child will see such a homemade doll as a lady attired in beautiful finery. Why? Because it stirs the imagination, and that induces movement in the inner organs, and it produces a feeling of well-being in the child. Notice how such a child plays in a lively and interested way, throwing body and soul into what the imagination conjures up, while the child with the perfect doll just sits, unexcited and unamused. It has no possibility to add anything through imagination, so the inner organs are condemned to inactivity. Children have an extraordinarily sound instinct for what is good for them, as long as only the physical body has become free to interact with the external world, and as long as they are in the process of development. Children will indicate what is beneficial to them. However, if from early on this instinct is disregarded, it will disappear. Education should be based on happiness, on joy and a child's natural cravings. To practice asceticism at this age would be synonymous with undermining healthy development.

When the child approaches the seventh year and the baby teeth are gradually being replaced, the covering of the ether body loosens and becomes free, as the physical body did at physical birth. Now the educator must bring everything that will further the development of the ether body. However, the teacher must guard against placing too much emphasis on developing the child's reason and intellect. Between the seventh and twelfth years, it is primarily a question of authority, confidence, trust, and reverence. Character and habit are special qualities of the ether body and must be fostered; but it is harmful to exert any influence on the reasoning faculty before puberty.

The development of the ether body occurs in the period from the seventh until the sixteenth year in boys, and until the fourteenth year in girls. It is important for the rest of a person's life that feelings of respect and veneration are fostered during this period. Such feelings can be awakened by means of information and narration—the lives of significant people can be depicted to children, not only from history, but from their own circle, perhaps that of a revered relative. Awe and reverence are awakened in children that forbid them to harbor any critical thoughts or opposition against the venerated person. The children live in solemn expectation of the moment they will be permitted to meet this person. Finally the day arrives and the children stand before the door filled with awe and veneration; they turn the handle and enter the room that, for them, is a holy place. Such moments of veneration become forces of strength in later life. It is immensely important that the educator, the teacher, is at this time a respected authority for the child. A child's faith and confidence must be awakened—not through axioms, but through human beings.

People around the children, with whom they have contact, must be their ideals; children must also choose such ideals from history and literature: "Everyone must choose the hero whose path to Olympus they will follow," is a true saying. The materialistic view that opposes authority and undervalues respect and reverence is totally wrong. It regards children as already self-reliant, but their healthy development is impaired if demands are made on the reasoning faculty before the astral body is born. At this time it is important that memory be developed. This is done best in a purely mechanical way. However, calculators should not be used; tables of multiplication, poems and so on should be committed to memory in a parrot-like fashion. It is simply materialistic prejudice to maintain that such things should be inwardly felt and understood at this age.

In the previous times educators knew better. Between the ages of one and seven all kinds of songs were sung to the children, such as the good old nursery rhymes and children's songs. Sense and meaning was not what mattered, but sound; the children were made aware of harmony and consonance, and we often find words inserted purely for the sake of their sound. Often the rhymes were meaningless. For example: "Fly beetle fly / your father is away / your mother is in Pommerland, Pommerland / fly beetle fly." Incidentally, in the idiom of children *Pommerland* meant motherland. The expression stemmed from a time when it was still believed that human beings were spiritual beings and had come down to Earth from a spiritual world. Pommerland was the land of spiritual origin. Yet it was not the meaning in such rhymes that was important, but the sound, thus, many children's songs made no particular sense.

This is the age when memory, habit and character must be established, and this is achieved through authority. If the foundation of these traits is not laid during this period, it will result in behavioral shortcomings later. Just because axioms and rules of conduct have no place in education until the astral body is born, it is important that prepubescent children, if they are to be properly educated, can look up to authority. Children can sense a person's innermost being, and that is what they revere in those with authority. Whatever flows from the educator to children forms and develops conscience, character and even the temperament—their lasting dispositions. During these years allegories and symbols act formatively on the ether body of children because such things manifest the world-spirit. Fairy tales, legends, and descriptions of heroes are a true blessing.

During this period, the ether body must receive as much care as the physical body. During the earlier period happiness and joy influenced the forming of the organs; from seven until fourteen—in this case boys until sixteen—the emphasis must be on everything that promotes feelings of health and vigor. Hence, the value of gymnastics. However, the desired effect will not be attained if the instructor aims at movements that solely benefit the physical body. It is important that the teacher can intuitively enter into how children inwardly sense themselves, and in this way to know which movements will promote inner sensations of health, strength, well-being, and pleasure in the bodily constitution. Only when gymnastic exercises induce feelings of growing strength are they of real value. More than the external aspect of the bodily nature benefits from correct gymnastic exercises; the way a person inwardly experiences the self also benefits.

Anything artistic has a strong influence on the ether body, as well as the astral body. Excellent vocal and instrumental music is particularly important, especially for the ether body. And there should be many objects of true artistic beauty in the child's environment.

Most important of all is religious instruction. Images of things supersensible are deeply imprinted in the ether body. The pupil's ability to have an opinion about religious faith is not important, but receiving descriptions of the supersensible, of what extends beyond the temporal. All religious subjects must be presented pictorially.

Great care must be taken that teaching is brought to life. Much is spoiled in the child if it is burdened with too much that is dull and lifeless. Whatever is taught in a lively interesting manner benefits the child's ether body. There should be much activity and doing, which has a quickening effect on the spirit. This is also true when it comes to play. The old kind of picture books have a stimulating effect because they contain figures that can be pulled by strings and suggest movement and inner life. Nothing has a more deadening effect on the child's spirit than putting together and fixing some structure, using finished geometrical shapes. That is why building blocks should not be used; the child should create everything from the beginning, learning to bring to life what is thus formed from the lifeless. Our materialistic age extinguishes life through mass-produced lifeless objects. Much dies in the young developing brain when the child has to do meaningless things like, for example, braiding. Talents are stifled and much that is unhealthy in our modern society can be traced back to the nursery. Inartistic lifeless toys do not foster trust in spiritual life. A fundamental connection exists between today's lack of religious belief and the way young children are taught.

When puberty is reached the astral covering falls away, and the astral body becomes independent. With the awakening feelings for the opposite sex, the ability to judge, to form personal opinion, also awakens. Only now should the reasoning faculty be appealed to—the critical intellect's approval or disapproval. This is not to say that one can form independent judgment the moment this age is reached, let alone earlier. It is absurd for such young people to judge issues or to have a say in cultural life. A young person under the age of twenty has a still undeveloped astral body, and can no more make sound judgments than a baby still in the womb can hear or see. Each life period requires a corresponding influence. In the first, it is a model to imitate; in the second an authority to emulate; the third requires rules of conduct, principles, and axioms. The *teacher* is of utmost significance for the young person at this time—the *personality* that will guide students' eagerness for learning and their desire for independence in the right directions.

Thus, the spiritual-scientific world-view provides an abundance of basic principles that help the teacher's task of developing and educating the young generations. We have shown that spiritual science can be applied to everyday life and is capable of practical intervention in important issues. We must understand all the members of the human being and how they interrelate in order to know when to influence which member in a truly beneficial way. The embryo will be affected if the expectant mother is not properly nourished; for its sake the mother must be cared for. Similarly, what later still surrounds and protects the child must also be cared for since this in turn will benefit the child. This holds true on both physical and spiritual levels. Therefore, as long as a child still slumbers as if within an etheric womb, and is still rooted in the astral covering, it is very important what happens in the environment. Children are affected by every thought, every feeling, every sentiment motivating those around them, even if not expressed. Here a person cannot maintain that one's thoughts and feelings do not matter as long as nothing is said.

Even in the innermost recesses of their hearts, those around the child cannot permit themselves base thoughts or feelings. Words affect only the external senses, whereas thoughts and feelings reach the protecting sheaths of the ether and astral bodies, and they pass over to the child. Therefore, as long as these protective coverings envelop the child, they must be cared for. Impure thoughts and passions harm them, just as unsuitable substances harm the mother's body.

Even subtle aspects are thus illumined by spiritual science. Through knowledge of the human being the educator gains the insight needed. Spiritual science does not intend to persuade; it is not a theory, it is practical knowledge applicable to life. Its effect is beneficial, for it makes human beings both physically and spiritually healthier. It provides effective truth that must flow into every aspect of life. There is no better way for spiritual science to serve humanity than fostering social impulses in the young during the formative years. What takes place in human beings during the time they grow up and mature is one of life's greatest riddles; those who find practical solutions will prove to be true educators.

Education and
Spiritual Science

BERLIN, JANUARY 24, 1907

Translated by Rita Stebbing

W H E N we discuss subjects such as that of today's lecture, we must keep before our mind's eye all of human evolution. Only then can we understand individual evolution and guide young people through education. At the center of education is the school. We shall attempt to understand what is required of education on the basis of human nature and a person's evolution in general.

We see the being of a person as consisting of four distinct members: physical body, ether or life body, astral body, and, at the center of one's being, the I. When an individual is born only the physical body is ready to receive influences from the external world. The ether body is not born until the time that the teeth change, and the astral body is not born until puberty is reached. The faculties of the ether body, such as memory, temperament, and so on, are, until the change of teeth, protected by an etheric sheath, just as the physical senses of eyes and ears are protected before physical birth by the maternal body. During this time the educator must not disturb what should develop naturally by itself.

Jean Paul expressed it by saying no world traveler learns as much on far-flung journeys as the child learns from the nurse before the age of seven. Why then must we have schools for children?

What evolves after the physical birth has occurred needs a protective covering, just as the embryo needs the maternal body's protection. The human being begins a life that is entirely new after a certain stage of development is reached. Until then life is a repetition of earlier epochs: the embryo repeats all the primordial stages of evolution up to the present, and after birth the child repeats earlier human evolutionary epochs.

Friedrich August Wolf[1] described the stages through which a human being evolves from childhood as follows: the first epoch, until the third year, he called the "golden, gentle, harmonious age," corresponding to the life of today's Indian and South Sea Islander. The second epoch, until the sixth year, reflects the Asiatic wars and their repercussions in Europe, and also the Greek heroic age, as well as the time of the native North American. The third epoch, until the ninth year, corresponds to the time from Homer[2] to Alexander the Great.[3] The fourth epoch, until the twelfth year, corresponds to the time of the Roman Empire. The fifth epoch lasts until the fifteenth year, when the inner forces should be ennobled through religion, and corresponds to the Middle Ages. The sixth epoch, until the eighteenth year, corresponds to the Renaissance. The

1. Friedrich August Wolf (1759–1824), German philologist and scholar of classicism, was a friend of Goethe. He contended that the *Iliad* and *Odyssey* are the work of more than one author.
2. Homer (8th or 9th century B.C.), Greek poet, traditionally considered the author of the *Iliad* and *Odyssey.*
3. Alexander III (356–323 B.C.), tutored by Aristotle, conquered many lands, and became king from 336–323 B.C.; he died of fever in Babylon.

seventh epoch lasts until the twenty-first year, corresponding to the Reformation; and the eighth epoch lasts until the twenty-fourth year, when a person reaches the present era.

This system is a valuable spiritual foundation, but it must be widened considerably to correspond to reality. It must include all of a human being's evolutionary descent. Human beings do not stem from the animal kingdom—though certainly from beings who were far below what human beings are today in physical development, they did not resemble apes in any way.

Spiritual science points back to a time when human beings inhabited Atlantis; compared to modern human beings, the Atlantean's soul and spirit were constituted differently.[4] Their consciousness could be called *somnambulistic*; the intellect was undeveloped—they could neither count nor write, and logical reasoning did not exist for them. But they beheld many aspects of the spiritual world. The will that flowed through their limbs was immensely strong. The higher animals such as apes were degenerate descendants of the Atlanteans.

Our dream consciousness is a residue of the Atlantean's normal pictorial consciousness, which could be compared with what a person experiences in vivid dreams during sleep. But the pictures of an Atlantean were animated, more vivid than today's most fertile imagination. Furthermore, Atlanteans could control their pictures, so that they were not chaotic. We see an echo of this consciousness when young children play, endowing their toys with pictorial content.

Human beings first descended into physical bodies during Lemurian time. That event is repeated during physical birth when, having descended into a physical body, a person begins

---

4. See *Cosmic Memory: Prehistory of Earth and Man*, Steinerbooks, Blauvelt, NY, 1990.

to develop through soul and spirit to higher levels. The Lemurian and Atlantean epochs are repeated in a child's development up to the seventh year. The epoch of evolution when great spiritual teachers appeared among humankind— Buddha, Plato, Pythagoras, Hermes, Moses, Zarathustra[5]—is repeated in the child between the change of teeth and puberty. In those days, the influence of the spiritual world was much greater, a fact we find preserved in heroic legends and sagas. It is therefore important that what is taught during this period of the child's life conveys the spirit of the earlier cultural epochs.

The period between the seventh and fourteenth years corresponds in the child to the time up to the twelfth century, the time when cities were founded. The main emphasis must now be on authority and community. The children should experience something of the power and glory that surrounded the early leaders. The most important issue that concerns a school, therefore, is the teacher. The teacher's authority must be self-evident for the children, just as what was taught by the great teachers was self-evident to the human soul. It is bad, it does great harm if the child doubts the teacher. The child's respect and reverence must be without reservation, so that the teacher's kindness and good will, which must be present naturally, seem to the child like a blessing. Pedagogical methods and principles are not what is important, but rather the teacher's profound psychological insight. The study of psychology is the most important subject of a teacher's training. An educator should not be concerned with how the human being ought to develop, but with the reality of how the student actually does develop.

---

5. See *Christianity as Mystical Fact and the Mysteries of Antiquity*, Rudolf Steiner Press, London, 1972.

Since every age makes different demands it is useless to lay down general rules. Knowledge or proficiency in pedagogical methods are not what matters in a teacher, but character and a certain presence that makes itself felt even before the teacher has spoken. The educator must have attained a degree of inner development, and must have become not merely learned, but inwardly transformed. The day will come when teachers will not be tested for knowledge, or even pedagogical principles, but for what they are as human beings.

For children the school must be their life. Life should not just be portrayed; former epochs must come to life. The school must create a life of its own, not draw it from outside. Human beings must receive at school what they will not be able to receive later in life. Pictorial and symbolic concepts must be fostered. The teacher must be deeply aware of the truth that "Everything transient is only appearance." When teachers present a subject pictorially, they should not be thinking it is merely allegory. If teachers fully participate in the life of the children, forces will flow from their soul to that of the children. Processes of nature must be described in rich imaginative pictures. The spiritual behind the sense-perceptible must be brought to life. Modern teaching methods fail completely in this regard, because only the external aspects are described. But a seed contains not only the future plant, it contains forces of the sun, indeed of the whole cosmos. A feeling for nature will awaken in the child when the capacity for imagery is fostered. Plants should not merely be shown and described, but rather the child should make paintings of them; then happy human beings for whom life has meaning will emerge from their time at school.

Calculators should not be used; one must do math with the children on living fingers. Vigorous spiritual forces must be stimulated. Nature study and arithmetic train the powers of thinking and memory; history the life of feeling. A sense for what is noble and beautiful awakens love for what is worthy of love. But what strengthens the will is religion; it must permeate the teaching of every subject. Children will not immediately grasp everything they are capable of absorbing; this is true of everyone. Jean Paul made the remark that one should listen carefully to the truth spoken by a child, but to have it explained one must turn to his or her parents. In our materialistic age too little is expected of memory. The child first learns; only later does it understand, and only later still will the underlying laws be understood.

Between the seventh and fourteenth years is also the time to foster the sense for beauty. Through this sense we grasp symbolic meaning. But most important is that the child is not burdened with abstract concepts; what is taught should have a direct connection with life. The spirit of nature—in other words the facts themselves existing behind the sense-perceptible—must have spoken to the child, who should have a natural appreciation of things before abstract theories are introduced; this should only be done after puberty. There is no need to be concerned that what is learned may be forgotten once school is finished; what matters is that what one teaches bears fruit and forms the character. What the child has inwardly experienced will also be retained; details may vanish but the essential, the universal, will remain and grow.

No education can be conducted without a religious foundation; school is an illusion without religion. Even Haeckel's *Riddle of the Universe* contains religion. No theory can ever replace religion, nor can a history of religion. A person of a basically religious disposition, who has deep conviction, will also be able to convey religion. The spirit that lives in the world also lives in human beings. Teachers must feel that they belong to a spiritual world-order from which a task is received.

There is a saying: A person's character is formed partly by study and partly by life. But school and education should not be something separate from life. It should be said, rather, that a person's character will be correctly formed when study is also life.

Interests, Talents, and Educating Children

NUREMBERG, NOVEMBER 14, 1910

Translated by Robert F. Lathe & Nancy Parsons Whittaker

WHEN outsiders consider the attitude and way of thinking of spiritual science and judge its content using the prevalent way of thinking they could easily conclude, somewhat correctly from their standpoint, that spiritual science creates high ideals out of thin air. Those ideals tend toward what outsiders might call "self-styled" knowledge of nature and the human soul and spirit. They might then say that those ideas and understandings are quite beautiful and satisfy the inner longings of the soul, and that it is understandable that those unconvinced by conventional science would be led to believe spiritual science the thirst of their souls. If someone familiar with spiritual science says something about the sense perceptible world or things in the conventional scientific domain, then an outsider might say it all sounds fantastic. That fantastic aspect is quite evident to an outsider. Those within spiritual science can easily understand how someone could find so much fantasy there. People with a conventional scientific perspective might easily say they cannot do anything with spiritual science. We can easily understand that.

In contrast, let us now consider someone who has penetrated spiritual science more deeply, who has gained insight into what the soul presents and has learned what the human soul and the human spirit actually are. Such a person will have quite different feelings. Such a person could look at the conventional view of the world and see what has arisen as its tasks, goals, and values, and how it has affected practical life. What materialism says about various areas of cultural activity seems quite fantastic to someone within spiritual science. For example, we need only hear what it has to say about education. To the spiritual researcher it simply sounds like a lot of slogans and clichés. We can look at the wide range of pedagogical effort and everywhere find sugar-coated words. Who has not heard, for example, "We should avoid stuffing things into children's souls," or, "We should develop human individuality"? But who can say anything beyond such extravagant slogans if *what human individuality is* has not been properly comprehended. In contrast to spiritual science, materialistic science is simply a sum of abstractions and, as such, is unrealistic. Someone who comprehends spiritual science must, therefore, reply that spiritual science not only wants to be practical, but also attempts to see the real foundation of things. That is possible particularly in the area of education.

If we use spiritual science to think imaginatively about a child, then, as we face the growing child living into life, we are overcome by the feeling that before us stands a sacred riddle. If we work with the child, we must seek to solve that riddle with a deep sense of reverence. We feel in that growing soul something different from everything we see. We feel that something unknown lives in the developing human being, and that feeling is correct. Our modesty and reverence cannot be great enough when we face the task of educating the child. Our humility before that being who presents us with a new riddle to solve can also not be great enough. I would not dare to speak about it if I had worked only with spiritual science. I do, however, dare to speak about it because, as a teacher, I have felt that sacred riddle for some fifteen years. From the modern standpoint, it is child's play not only to deride such things but, also with an apparent right, to refute as fantastic the idea of human reincarnation and the reappearance of people in new lives. Today, we will only mention in passing the idea of reincarnation, that our embodied souls living today through the period between birth and death have *often* gone through life. We will only mention that we live today so that later we can experience the effects and fruits of this life. People can easily refute that in theory. However, things look different when you teach with the correct feelings and see how the growing soul of the child develops from week to week and from year to year. If you approach your desire to teach with the proper attitude, then you will recognize that you will be affecting something developed over millennia. If you consider everything children do and everything you do from that perspective, then you can see how fruitful education can be. Those who know the laws of logical proof know the impossibility of proving this point of view through formal logic. However, if you *work* with this in mind, then you will feel the truth.

We certainly confront a difficult task when we want to understand how the child's soul develops. Everyone knows the purely external facts. However, who has not experienced how powerless teachers often are when the law or parents' demands define their tasks? Who has not experienced the frustration when the assigned tasks contradict the child's innate interests and talents? Who has not felt and seen the truth that even the greatest efforts achieve nothing if we do not take the child's aptitudes into account? How often life has shown us that we are powerless not only before the child's lack of ability, but also before our own lack of understanding. We attempt to educate, but if we educate improperly, the effects are not immediately visible. However, if we follow a student's life, we often see something quite curious, namely, that talents and predispositions later arise from the child's soul only after difficult struggles. Then we can see that had we only recognized them and been more helpful, we could have spared the child much that occurred later. We see how necessary it is to focus upon the difficult question of the child's innate interests and gifts, and that we must take them into account in our teaching. People are very unclear about such basic questions today, because modern ideas and concepts inevitably numb people. One such concept is that of heredity, but such concepts form people's entire attitude. When speaking of a child's aptitudes, who would not first think of asking how much the child inherited from his or her parents and ancestors? Goethe once spoke of that with understandable modesty, but in a way based upon a deep awareness:

> From Father I have stature,
> For the seriousness of life,
> From Mother a happy nature
> And a love for storytelling.

After relating a few other things about heredity, he closes with:

> What now lives in the little imp
> That can still be called original?[1]

Posterity has already given a partial answer and will continue to answer in future generations. Someone who has spent some twenty years studying Goethe certainly has a right to say something. With all due respect to the Frankfurt councilman from

---

1. Wolfgang Johannes Goethe, *Zahme Xenien* (Gentle satires), volume VI, No. 32.

whom Goethe inherited his stature for the seriousness of life...
If you look at how Goethe led his life, you will certainly have
respect for what he inherited from his father. If you look at the
agile and caring way his mother looked at life and interacted
with people, then you will certainly see what Goethe wants to
say he inherited from his mother. What is the result if you put
these together? If you put them together and think about it,
you will find that what he could not have inherited is his effectiveness. What could *not* be inherited is Goethe himself and
what the Guiding Forces allowed to stream into him and used
to express themselves. It is the same with everyone as it is with
great people. You cannot move forward if you try to attribute
everything to heredity without considering the individual, who
develops according to its own laws. Thus, if you consider life
objectively the question becomes less simple—that is, what is
the relationship between what we can trace back to our ancestors and what is obviously there, what is personal?

Spiritual science certainly does not deny inherited characteristics, but how does it view heredity? You can, of course, see
"heredity" everywhere. There are people who claim that when
characteristics appear that cannot be found in the ancestors, we
can still point to heredity because those abilities may have been
present previously, though undeveloped. This is often said and
often disputed. People who speak this way have only a vague
concept of innate capacities, which is not realistic because they
invent explanations for everything. It seems to me that someone
who does that is the same as one who says that every brick has a
tendency to fall on people's heads. It just needs someone to be
there. One who thinks realistically certainly cannot speak of
innate capacities in that way. The task of a genuine pedagogy is
to separate the hereditary from the nonhereditary. By using
an example from the animal kingdom, we can create a picture
of heredity. A chicken egg contains the whole "seed" of the

chicken, but it needs heat from *outside*. Therefore, we can see that heat is a basic element but does not exist in the "seed" itself. Nevertheless, superficial observation will show that animals can inherit certain things, whereas when we speak of human beings, we must certainly admit that there are some things we cannot inherit. Think of what we call instinct. It is unquestionably in the animal from the very beginning, so we must consider it to be inherited. Because an animal is part of a whole species and inherits all of the characteristics of that species; its manual skill, for example, is much greater than that of human beings. Human beings are much worse off than animals in that way.

People who speak with humility customarily create humble concepts. Those who speak with pride create proud concepts; they tend to say that animals are lower than human beings. This is not true in an absolute sense. For instance, anyone can read about how long it took human intelligence to develop paper, but wasps developed it long before that. If we study the animal kingdom, then we can see how ostensibly intellectual activities develop from simple instincts. However, we may not then conclude that human beings are less intelligent than animals. People cannot inherit certain things. Everyone would agree that a wasp inherits the skill to construct its nest; however, there can be no doubt that a human being set in the wilderness would never develop language or self-awareness. Human beings cannot inherit speech and self-awareness. Heredity does not contain them. People must always learn them anew. Thus, even superficial observation shows that we cannot address the most important things for humanity in the same way as we do those of the animal kingdom. On the other hand, who could deny the existence of things that we can inherit? Who would deny Schopenhauer's statement that he inherited much of his thoughtful character from his mother and much of the nature of his will from his father? Who would deny that there is something important and truthful in that, even if awkwardly expressed? We can see that human beings do, in fact, enter earthly existence with inherited characteristics, and it is our task to differentiate those inherited traits from those not inherited. This is what experience shows us. Nevertheless, someone could agree that we do not inherit speech and self-awareness, but that we still do not need to make such subtle distinctions because everything will work out. When a human being is born into a particular linguistic region, he or she will learn to speak.

Are there other nonhereditary characteristics, whose source we must seek at a deeper level in the human personality? It is not so easy to differentiate those nonhereditary traits and talents within human nature from hereditary ones. Clearly, it is heredity when seven musicians are born to the Bach family. Nevertheless, those who approach education realistically can do nothing other than separate the essence of the individual from what is inherited. We must be very clear about the role of heredity.

We see that when a child enters earthly existence, he or she is more like the father in some ways and more like the mother in others. We see the child has certain characteristics from the mother and others from the father. Someone who considers life objectively will soon notice that there is, in fact, a difference between what the father gives to the child and what the mother gives. Of course, these things intermingle, but we can differentiate between the elements coming from the mother and those coming from the father. If you look more closely, the distribution of these two factors becomes clear. We can see that all the inherited characteristics related to the quality of intelligence and the capacity for reason can in some way be traced back to some characteristics of the mother. The traits we can summarize as *steadfastness* of *character,* strength and an ability to enter into life, which have a will-like quality—whether in the son or in the daughter—can be traced back to characteristics of the father.

Notice, I did not say that we can trace the child's intelligence back to the intelligence of the mother, but that we can trace it back to the *nature* of the mother's intelligence, and that we can trace the child's steadfastness back to the *nature* of the father's character.

If you look at these things in more detail, you will soon see significant differences between the course of the parents' lives and the nature of the child's life, particularly regarding whether a child is born early or late in the marriage. An educator can see quite different relationships of the child to the parents depending upon whether the child is born early or late in the marriage. Observation shows that in children born later in the marriage, when the parents have already had experience in their work, the mother's or father's characteristics are much more strongly represented, and the children bear the imprint of the parents much more clearly. In that case, there is greater intellectual flexibility and a more firmly contoured character. It is interesting to consider children in this manner when we attempt to answer the question of what heredity carries.

Heredity is an expression of prior processes in the physical world. What is hereditary? Hereditary characteristics are genuinely part of the physical body. If we say characteristics of intelligence are hereditary, then we must say these are connected with the physical body—that is, the brain. Since we are given that instrument, it is natural that we show hereditary characteristics. We inherit the finer details of our organs, and we must accept them. In this way we can explain our dependencies on those organs since we inherit them. To make a gross comparison, if you are born with one hand you will see how much you depend on it. Essentially, it is always the physical body that comes into consideration when we speak of heredity as I have done here. What practical observations of life reveal as the *core* of our being crystallizes from that, and we are unable to understand it if we trace it back to heredity. The child is born with a certain intellectual flexibility, with a capacity to reason; we can look at the mother and see that it originates with her. We study the child's character and then look at the father and can gain some insight about it.

However, something special remains that is the most important thing for the educator, since only when we can bring it into harmony with inherited traits can education be successful. We can trace the way reason develops back to the mother, but the quality of reasoning indicates particular realms of life, and we cannot trace that back to the mother. The characteristics of one mother will show us a tendency toward music, those of another toward mathematics. It would be a great error to direct intelligence everywhere. The quality of intelligence is hereditary, but we cannot inherit the particular direction, the talent for this or that, although it is contained within the kind of intelligence. Thus, as teachers, our task is to look at the mother and comprehend the flexibility of intelligence, for instance, why a child thinks slowly or quickly. But we must also recognize the child's specifically individual tendency toward this or that. We can clearly see the characteristics inherited from the father in a different way. We can understand the child's steadfastness of character and certainty of will when we look at the father. However, one thing we cannot so easily understand is the *direction* of interest that crystallizes out of the core of the child's being. We see in one child one direction of interest and in another child, another. These are specific to the individual.

To proceed wisely as educators, we must ask how the mother's way of reasoning and the father's character traits present themselves. If we are to properly educate, we must recognize *interests* lying within the child's *character* and the *direction of intelligence*. We can easily confuse these. That is why the father has so much difficulty raising a child who is particularly like him. And the other way around, when a child is particularly like the mother, the mother has great difficulty with the child. Children who are particularly like their father are more easily raised by the mother, and children who are particularly like their mother are more easily raised by the father. If a child is like the father, then he or she has the will impulses of the father. However, the father cannot transfer his interests to the child. The child's talents arise within the realm of the mother with the result that, in this area, the father can understand very little of the child. The child will hone itself on the father's character, but the mother can best care for the child's talents. In the reverse case, when the child is more like the mother, it will be difficult for the mother to follow the child's interest in the way the father can. The golden rule is: Talents form in all quietude, character in the rush of the world! Talents develop in the loving care of the mother, character in the firm care of the father.

Usually, we do not meet people who clearly present the mixture of characteristics inherited from the mother and the father. Generally, either the father's or the mother's influence predominates. A very important rule for teaching follows from that. Suppose the motherly element predominates. Then, we can often see how much the child seems like the mother and can easily guess his or her specific talent. However, when the fatherly element has been pushed aside, we will have considerably more difficulty finding the particular interests that lie within what the child has inherited from the father. In that case, as teachers we must look at what heredity has not accomplished. We must look particularly closely at the father to see whether he is easygoing or rigid. Then, we must develop the repressed inherited characteristics. We can do that if we direct our attention toward the other side. We will soon discover the child's talents and capabilities, but what heredity does *not* provide, we must achieve through *education*. What should the educator do? Here we have something of tremendous importance: When the teacher sees that something the child could have inherited from the father is not clearly apparent, then he or she must work to direct the child's talents; the child's attention must be directed toward tasks and *activities* consistent with the child's talents. The talents must be captivated by external objects. Children who are more like the mother must become accustomed to being surrounded by objects consistent with their talents, toward which their attention can be directed. It is not appropriate to follow the rule that, because children have interests, they should be allowed to simply follow them.

Suppose a child is particularly like the father. Then we will have difficulty guessing what his or her talents and capacities are, but the child's interests will be clearly expressed through the will. The interests will live in the *strength* of the child's desires. We must be particularly careful not to base our conclusions about the child's real talents upon his or her interests. In this case, we must carefully study the child's interests in the proper manner. If we allow interests to mature for which no talent exists, we harm the child. An interest of the soul for which there is no corresponding talent will turn upon the soul. This constantly causes illness and disturbs the physical nervous system. Many such cases can be traced back to people's lack of understanding about how to harmonize interests with talent. We can learn much by seeing how children's impulsive expressions of particular interests lead to awkwardness and, on the other hand, how other interests lead to gracefulness. We give this little attention, but we should carefully classify interests. Furthermore, as a teacher you have the task of restraining interests that would lead to awkwardness. You can best accomplish that if you ask how the father and the mother are. You must then discover the essence of the child's nature that crystallized out of the heritage of the mother and the father. We can truly say, therefore, that education must be based on knowledge, not on slogans like "Educate in harmony" or "Consider the individual." Just try to educate harmoniously when you don't know where interests lead, or try to emphasize the individual when you don't know how to find what is specific to the individual!

This is only one aspect of education, however. Human beings come into the world not just for their own sake, but also for the sake of humanity. We cannot simply accept what appears in the child. The teacher will soon notice a complementary relationship that we in spiritual science call the laws of karma. You can easily see that beings are placed where they have something to do in the world. Edelweiss does not grow in the plains, but upon the mountaintops. Everything grows within its own element and cannot thrive where it does not belong. It is the same with the essence of the human being, which places itself in that element where it belongs. Things are more harmonious than we might think. For this reason, talents are more in harmony with those of the mother and interests more with those of the father. Nevertheless, we must also look in the other direction. Human beings depend upon the fact that individuals do not speak their own private languages but the language of the area where they are born. That is, they are dependent upon the people in their surroundings. Thus, an entire manner of thinking and feeling enters deeply into the soul through language. That is coarsely observable. Compare the soul of someone from Frankonia with that of someone from West Prussia,[2] and then try to see how language affects the entire manner of thinking and perceiving. It is that way with everything, namely, people are placed into life according to their qualities. Thus, if we want to educate consciously, we

2. Translators' note: This would be comparable in contemporary United States to comparing someone raised in Louisiana with someone from New York.

must know that we do not educate people only as individuals. Just as we cannot provide each child with an individual language, so we also cannot do something special for each child. Human nature is organized so that people adapt to the existing cultural process. We must raise children in what belongs to *humanity*, and it must take root in them.

When this becomes apparent to us, we must acknowledge powerlessness against those elements. If we look at the child's talents and then at the demands of life, it might appear impossible for us to bring them into harmony. Let us look at two children. One child is born in an environment and learns a particular language. He or she grows up with that language and it becomes a part of his or her soul, a part of the innermost human being. Anyone who has thought about the relationship of language to human nature will know that through language people learn not only how to reason logically, but also how to reason through feeling. For example, the way the *a* or *u* sound works in a language tremendously effects the soul's capacity to *feel*. Language provides a "skeleton" for feelings and perceptions. Imagine another child who, due to life's events, had to learn another language immediately after barely learning his or her mother language. Compare this child with one who is totally integrated with his or her language, so that not only is thinking done in that language, but also the child has learned to be in it. Then you will see that the soul life of this second child is much less settled and much less solid. A language that forms a skeleton for the soul results in a sounder nature. A language that "carries" the soul makes the soul less stable and less certain. Thus, the soul of a child who develops in the latter way is much more easily irritated, and does not meet life's external influences as vigorously.

Language can teach us the great importance of connecting educational principles and what later becomes the content of life with what occurs earlier. Everything inconsistent in education significantly destroys the life of the soul. When we fail to build upon what occurred earlier, we inflict the greatest damage upon the soul. In contrast, a conscious connection has a marvelous effect. If you often sit with a child with a weak character and begin, so that the child does not notice, to speak about things that happened three years before, you can more easily reprimand the child than when you refer to events of the present. You can strengthen the child's character by using memories of earlier occurrences. We commit major errors if we attempt to correct the child through punishment or controls that arise out of our present anger. We can easily make mistakes when the deed is fresh. Life is not without contradiction and people must make errors; however, we can correct them. If you need to correct, then sit with the child and speak about an earlier misbehavior, since the child is past it and no longer feels what occurred earlier. Feelings become numb and go a very different way than thoughts and memory. We see that we can objectively discuss things that occurred earlier, and the more often we do that and refresh the child's memory of what happened, the more we can *develop character.* These are simply rules that result from objective observations.

Of course, you need a spiritual-scientific view to gather the individual events together. But then you can understand them and draw important conclusions. We must look not only at the individual, but at the whole. Then we must look toward creating harmony between individual nature and human nature. If you return to past events it is possible to bring out a certain kind of sympathy. You will, for example, find it difficult to bring selfishness into harmony with the demands of the surroundings. However, if you go back to past experiences, then you will notice that you can engage the child. The educator must bring earlier experiences into harmony with what occurs later. Teachers must be careful to bring individual children into harmony with the demands of all humankind by working with past occurrences. The more you reach back into the child's previous experiences, the better you can teach. This is how you should look for what is good for educating children.

We are amiss in allowing obvious talent to go undeveloped and by placing children in continuous contradiction to their surroundings; this causes illness. Suppressed talents and interests slip into people's inner being, and later, can result in illnesses of the soul. We sin against human health if we allow children's interests to go undeveloped. We are also amiss to neglect the adjustment of children to their surroundings. If we fail to do this a contradiction between the child's soul and life's demands will cause a deep dissatisfaction with life. One who understands the human soul could say that all the interests that should have been nurtured, and all the talents that should have been developed are missing in those who wander through life saying how difficult life is. This results in people who cannot find their way in life and become dissatisfied as a result.

Now you could easily say that everything I have said relates to inner soul characteristics found within the intellect and the will. However, those are the most important things for the educator since they show the essence of the soul, and this is where teachers can create the most misfortune. How is that? The development of interests and talents results in a kind of fluidity of reasoning at an early stage, but at thirty years of age, it becomes a dexterity in the fingers and hands. Awkwardness at the age of thirty can be traced back to the fact that flexible thinking was not learned around age seven. The lack of participation that occurs if we do not develop interests reveals itself as indifference in all manner of practical responsibilities. We must recognize that the core of human nature expresses itself in those character traits.

A spiritual scientist would recommend that a child play. Why do children play, and why should they play? Here I want to say something about later life. You all certainly are aware of something that occurs in life, namely, being tired. However, where does fatigue arise? You often hear the reply that fatigue occurs in the evening when the muscles are worn out. Is it true that the muscles, due to their nature, come into a state of fatigue? If that were so, then we could certainly ask how tired the muscles in our heart would be. They would certainly need to rest. It is not in the nature of muscles to become tired. Muscles do what they need to do. They do not become tired. External activity does not affect the muscles of the heart. Fatigue arises only when you make your muscles do something related to the external world, something connected with conscious activity. Disharmony between the demands of the outer world and our muscles causes fatigue. The truth is that fatigue arises only because of a disharmony between our inner constitution and the outer world. Fatigue shows that a certain contradiction exists between the outer world and inner life. You must be aware that the human cultural process proceeds not only according to laws implanted in the individual constitution.

The nature of the human soul is directed not only toward the preservation of the species, but also toward the development of soul and spirit. Here, two streams are expressed: progress and organic structure. In the eternal laws of existence it is written that human beings must sacrifice purely natural laws to spiritual laws. Those who understand these things will not complain, but will comprehend entirely that a counterbalance is necessary. We must have a healthy preparation for life so that we can act on external things with our hands and think about external things with our brains. We must create a balance that is possible only when we are in a position to do things at a particular time that the outer world does not require and to be satisfied with the activity itself. Human nature meets that need through playing. It is best for the child if we allow play to be individually oriented, since that creates inner strength. If we structure play, then you will certainly see what results. Today, people want to standardize everything. Modern people cannot even admit that we need clothing cut to the individual. A basic tendency of modern culture is that we should feed even the most extreme followers of Nietzsche from the same pot.[3] We should not introduce standardization into the upbringing of children, especially not in play. We must allow play to be individualistic. We must give special attention to what the talents and interests of each child are, for otherwise we would sin. That brings us, as practicing teachers, to the need to believe that it is the child's spirit and not the muscles that must have the strength to resist wear and tear. Spirit and soul must be independent in play so that material things have no effect. Thus, in play children can remain unaffected by the tiring influences of the outer world. If we do not believe in an inwardly free soul, we cannot teach effectively.

If you really work that way, however, you will see something important. You will recognize that in childhood we must be free of the coarsely material laws of the world. The earlier you apply such rules to the child, the more you bring the child to a state in which playing is no longer a "free activity." Children need truths they can embrace with heart and soul, so they need not be slaves to what occurs in the outer world. This is why you should tell fairy tales and myths that go into the soul. In that way, you can create inner truths that free the soul. Previously, humanity did that instinctively, but in our time it is necessary to be more conscious of the need to do it.

---

3. Translators' note: Nietzsche's core value was that of extreme individualism.

Now, someone might ask how a teacher could recognize a child's particular talents. That is really not so difficult. One of the basic characteristics of a teacher, as I mentioned in a more comprehensive manner, is modesty before what is struggling to free itself as the essence of an individual. If we are humble before something that has been developing for thousands of years, something that we must help develop further, we will feel a responsibility that brings life to our souls. It gives us a particular quality, it gives us a stroke of genius. Teachers often have no idea why they do the right things. Children say what they need. The most important thing that we need in the education profession is the love that results when we learn to love the personality just beginning to develop. We will see what this love can accomplish with the spirit. In outer life, love is often blind. However, when we connect love to inner development, then it acts to open the soul. Behind that love exists a still more powerful belief, which acts on us to create the capacity to consider life in the proper manner, and which reveals to us the human being placed into the world of spiritual and sense perceptible life. As teachers, our task is to create the connection between those two. We see in the child how the spirit descends and weds human physicality. When we see that, when we see how the spirit weds human physicality in the child, our teaching will express what we can call a true belief in life, and this can be expressed as follows:

> The richness of matter
> impinges upon the human senses
> from the mysterious depths of the cosmos;
> The clear light of the spirit
> floods into the depths of the soul
> from the heights of the cosmos.
> They unite within the human being
> to create wisdom-filled reality.

Interests, Talent,
and Education

BERLIN, JANUARY 12, 1911

Translated by Robert F. Lathe & Nancy Parsons Whittaker

IF we look at what runs as a kind of *leit motif* through the previous winter lectures, and at the living essence of human beings living not only between one birth and death but in repeated earthly lives, then we must ask, "What shapes a human being during one earthly life and has particular significance in modern times?" Modern people certainly question and try to understand the relationship between innate interests and talents, and education. However, since people have little inclination to turn their gaze from what appears to be formative, and direct it toward the Creator of human beings, their questions easily take on an incomplete and vague character. If you assume that human nature contains something that gives life and exists throughout many lifetimes, you will recognize the complexity of questions concerning the essence of the human being. You will want to consider questions about innate interests, talent, and education in a new light, which is very different from simply considering what modern people so often emphasize—that is, heredity, or characteristics inherited from ancestors.

Spiritual science does not deny the existence of such inherited traits, nor does it ignore anything that can be learned from careful observation or through external senses and intellectual considerations. However, spiritual science recognizes how all of that relates to and serves the essence of the human being. This human essence absorbs it in the same way that matter in physical life supports the tiny seed of a living plant as it determines its form out of itself. What makes it possible for that plant being to create its form externally is the substance, the matter, it absorbs from its surroundings. Thus, in the general way a human being lives, we will need to recognize a connection between what comes into existence through birth and the essence of the individual human being from which a human being draws its spiritual and soul nutrition.

If, for example, we realize that our tasks as teachers are connected to a human soul that steps into earthly existence and, from hour to hour and week to week, increasingly develops its inner capacities, and if we stand before a growing human being as before a sacred riddle to be solved, a being who has come to us from the endless distances of the cosmos so that we can give that being the possibility to unfold and develop, then many new tasks, outlooks, and possibilities will arise for all of human life. We thus see a human being entering existence through birth and assume that, in a certain sense, that being's essential nature is brought into earthly existence through birth. Conventional science shows us—if we ignore slogans and theories and look instead to the facts—how spirit and soul essence of the human being works on within the child after birth, and how what appears to us as physical structure is changed and fashioned under the influence of the spirit-soul.

Conventional science can also show us, for example, how we should initially view the tool for external activity, the brain. It shows us that the human brain is still undefined and very pliable when human beings first enter earthly existence through birth. It shows us how the child then endeavors to absorb the cultural treasures of its environment and how that treasure shapes and creates the brain like an artist working with pliable material. As I have often mentioned in other connections, a newborn human being left helpless on a deserted island could not acquire the ability to speak. We must then say that the spirit and soul content of language comes to us after birth and does not arise from within the human being. It is not something connected only with a person's character or received without the influences of the environment, as with the second set of teeth. Speech acts on the human being. It is truly a sculptor that fashions the human brain. Through conventional science, we can follow the formation of the child's brain during the first period of life and even over years. Even if we can offer anatomical or physiological proof that the human capacity to speak and to remember linguistic concepts is connected with one or another organ, and that we collect every word in something like a library book, we would still have to ask, "What initially formed the brain that way?" The answer is: the spirit and soul content of the language spoken in the person's environment.

This shows us that, when considering human soul development, we must differentiate people's thoughts, ideas and perceptions, and also the feelings and tendencies of will that remain simple inner experiences, from what persists as such a strong inner experience, to the degree that it affects the external physical form and sculpts it as a future tool for intellectual capacities, or soul-spiritual life. We can best illustrate this when we follow human capacities over a lifetime, follow the very different aspects, although psychology often mixes these differing aspects together. We can best illustrate this by looking at our memory.

When we absorb something into our memory, when we memorize, we use something that has repetition as one of its primary characteristics. We have made what we memorized our own and can repeat it. Now, everyone has had the unfortunate experience of forgetting. We forget things and they disappear from memory so that we can no longer recall them later. Or don't you remember how much you had to memorize and recite in your youth? But, does everything we have memorized disappear completely?

We now want to look at what it means when people say they have forgotten something—that is, when they can no longer recall something well enough to repeat it. Has it vanished? It is there in a way similar to something I already mentioned, something we normally forget—that is, the wonderful, rich first experiences of childhood. We can remember back only to a certain point in childhood. However, before that moment we had an endless number of impressions. Who would not acknowledge this when considering the first years of a child's development? Nevertheless, those things are forgotten in the sense that we normally speak of forgetting. But have they completely disappeared? Do they cease to play any role in the human soul? No, they play a significant role in the human soul. A great deal depends on our first childhood impressions—whether our experiences are joyful or sad, filled with love or indifference. Much of the total attitude of adult souls depends, more than people usually suppose, on those early experiences. What formed and developed our soul during those first years, but that we have forgotten, is more important than people will usually admit.

The same is true of what we learn later. We forget the exact words and the exact thoughts, but they remain in our souls as a kind of mood. If, for example, someone at a particular age learns ballads or other poems about the tasks and qualities of great heroes, then that person might forget the thoughts and details, and no longer be able to recite them. What one learned, though, remains in the composition of the character, perhaps as strength in the soul or as a way to face life, to bear joy and sorrow. The things we forget lead to moods, feelings, even to will-impulses. They lead to what rests more or less consciously within our souls, but works and creates within us.

Sometimes through particular events later in life, we find that something we thought forgotten is actually not quite forgotten. We see that in certain circumstances, when there is an event related to something in their soul, that people remember something they thought was forgotten. In this way, we can show that we had simply covered over what we forgot with layers of subconscious soul, and that it still exists. In fact, we can see how what we forget, what has slipped from memory, works to form and develop our souls and reveals itself in our moods of joy and sorrow, in our courage, our bravery or cowardice, or often in our fear and anxiety. As things slip from memory and sink into the subconscious, they act creatively on our souls. We are essentially made up of what we have forgotten. Seen concretely, what are human beings other than *how* they are joyful or courageous, and so forth? If we look at people as they manifest, not abstractly, then we must say that they are the harmonious interweaving and interplaying of their characteristics, so that they are the result of what seeps into the deeper layers of their consciousness. That is what we see during life.

From everything we have discussed, and what we have yet to mention, we can see that what has sunk into deeper layers goes even deeper when people pass through the gates of death. Whenever human beings form their physical being during life with what they have received, they find a particular organic structure already present. Those structures have certain characteristics when the person enters life, and the creative forces in the soul must work against them. Suppose that we could develop courage through something we absorb. If, however, we have a cowardly constitution rather than a courageous one, then we must struggle somewhat against our own constitution. When we go through the period between death and rebirth, the essential activity of that period of human development is the preparation of the prototype or "protoform" of our new physical body—that is, the preparation of our new physical earthly body. During that time, we do not have the boundaries and resistance that limit our constitution between birth and death. With what we have achieved during earthly life, we work there as sculptors on the "whys" and "wherefores" of a new physical body with much greater freedom than is possible between birth and death. Thus, the ideas we forget during life between birth and death work upon our souls, and when we pass through the gates of death, these forgotten ideas work on the fabric of our next constitution until our rebirth. They work into everything connected with our new bodily configuration. Thus, through birth we enter a new existence, with tendencies reaching much deeper levels of our being than the ideas forgotten during life between birth and death could reach.

You can understand from this that, since human beings base a new bodily constitution on their immediate surroundings, each person later uses again those conditions in a particular way. It is different with animals, as we have seen in the lectures "Human and Animal Souls" and "Human and Animal Spirit."[1] Heredity determines their constitution. Animals have very specific willing tendencies because they do not take those tendencies from their environment. Recall how little an animal learns through training and thus how little it needs a place in the

---

1. See Rudolf Steiner's lectures "*Menschenseele und Tierseele*" (November 10, 1910) and "*Menschengeist und Tiergeist*" (November 17, 1910) in *Antworten der Geisteswissenschaft auf die grossen Fragen des Daseins* (Spiritual-scientific answers to the great questions of existence) GA 60 (untranslated).

physical world to express what has been received as formative principles. Human beings, however, need such a place, and for that reason enter the world awkwardly, but in such a way that they need only balance the finer details of their constitution. Human individuality springs from a person's own basic essence in the first years of existence. That is why the organ of the mind, the brain, is still pliable at birth, and only afterward receives its final and decisive paths, the lines and directions of how its tendencies should develop further.

When we consider development to be a result of earlier stages of existence, we see it is less important that we have specific educational standards than that we view each individual human being as a question, as a sacred riddle to be solved. We see that we have the responsibility to create the opportunities to solve that riddle in the best way possible. An education without firm rules, one that must appeal to artistically applied principles of teaching in order to develop the essential qualities of a human being, is bothersome. It is certainly more bothersome than if we rigidly say that we should develop one or another capacity. We have the proper attitude toward a growing human being, however, only when we consider each child as an individual, as special. If you want to take this in a trivial way—and today people have a gift for reducing everything to trivia—then you could say that individuality is visible not only in human beings, but also in every animal. That is certainly true, and no one speaking from a spiritual-scientific perspective would deny it. I have often said that if you want to speak of individuality in that sense, then you must look more closely at things, and be aware that if you want trivia, then you could also talk about the biography and individuality of a feather pen. I once knew a man who could distinguish feather pens according to their maker, because in his day people cut their pens from goose feathers and in this way had a personal relationship to the feather. Since he had a good imagination, he could easily think up a detailed biography for each feather pen. With people, however, we do not need to use that level of triviality. We must rather take our yardstick from the depths of cognition.

Such observations show us how people sculpt and create their personality, appearance and constitution, and how their essence exists within them. We can see from the way they live how human beings use what they receive from their surroundings, from what occurs during the first years of life, and how human development transforms and reforms them. It is particularly important during the first years of life that we nurture children's capacity to modify their physical constitution in a flexible way, that we do not repress their adaptability. We repress those capacities most if we prematurely stuff children with concepts and ideas that relate only to external perceptions with sharply delineated contours, or when we tie them to activities anchored in particular theoretical forms. In such cases, there is no variability, no modification, not even the possibility of developing spiritual and soul capacities so that the soul can act day to day and hour to hour. Suppose that a father was particularly stubborn and decided that his son must be just like him. "Throughout my life I have made shoes for my customers in this way; my son must do exactly the same. The way I think is exactly the way my son must think." The son lives in a spiritual and soul environment that acts on his own spiritual and soul constitution in the same way that the father's was worked on, and the son is, therefore, forced into specific constitutional forms. However, we need to discover the individual living in the son so that his constitution can be formed accordingly.

The human instinct for education has created a wonderful common means of enabling young children to work on changing, modifying, and mobilizing what lives in their spirit-soul, thus providing free space for the formation of human nature.

That means is play. That is also the way we can best occupy a child. We should not give children concepts with fixed boundaries, but rather ideas that allow the freedom to think about them, so that children can err here and there. That is the only way we can find the predestined path of thinking arising from each child's innate interest. Tell a fairy tale to excite the child's mental activity. Do not tell it so that fixed concepts develop, but so that the concepts remain flexible. A child will then work the way someone works who tries this and that, and by trying tries to discover what is proper. A child works to discover how the spirit must move to best shape his or her particular constitution according to inner predetermination. That is how play works. Play differs from activities with more fixed forms because children can still, to a certain extent, do what they want when playing. From the start, play has no clearly defined contours in the children's thoughts, nor any clearly defined movement in their organs. Through play, children have a free but definable manner of acting upon the human soul constitution. Play and the accompanying soul activity of the young child arise from a deep consciousness of what truly constitutes the nature and essence of the human being. Those who would be a real teacher must be fully aware that they must study, recognize, and identify every capacity in each of their students. However, there are certain basic principles that show us how the human essence that goes from birth to birth uses what is external to it—that is, what is in the line of heredity.

It is particularly interesting to look at the very different ways that the essence of a human being uses the characteristics, virtues, and so on, from the mother and father, and from the ancestors of the mother and father, to create something new. The essence of each human does not always use the parents' characteristics in the same way, but there is a basic determining principle, which is very illuminating. If we attempt to completely comprehend it, to have full insight in that regard, then we must see that there are two viable aspects of the human soul. One is the intellect, including our capacity to imagine things pictorially—whether quickly or slowly, or more or less wisely—and the other aspect lies in the general direction of willing and feeling—that is, our interest in our surroundings. The entire way in which we can accomplish something depends on whether we have a quick or a slow mind, a mind that can more or less penetrate things—that is, whether we are reasonably astute. What we can do for others and how we accomplish it depends upon whether we know how to connect our interests properly with what happens around us. Many people have good intent, but little interest in their surroundings or in other people; in such cases, interest cannot bring forth capacities. We must, therefore, consider the question of interest just as much as the question of whether the intellect is flexible enough to allow us to do one thing or another for our fellow human beings.

By interest, we mean everything connected with how people express their desires, how they act, whether they develop gracefully or awkwardly—in other words, everything connected with the life of the soul and with our interaction with the outer world, with our strong or weak interests and our capacities. People inherit the most important characteristics of interest from the father, so that what arises from those interests—the capacity for what arises from those interests, the capacity to use our organs and our entire being—is inherited, in general, from the father. The soul takes the corresponding aspects from the father, so that we can develop those characteristics. In contrast, intellectual flexibility, including imaginative activity, pictorial thinking, and a capacity to discover, is brought into earthly existence through birth as an inheritance of the mother's characteristics. You will find this particularly interesting thought indicated in a certain way by Schopenhauer.[2] He had an idea of it, but was not in a position to bring out the deeper aspects.

On the other hand, we may also say something else. Living in the father, as the way he relates to things, is his interests and desires, what he expects, wishes, or wants, whether he acts courageously or timidly avoids life, whether he is pedantic or expansive—in short, those qualities connected with tendencies of will; a child receives all those characteristics, in a sense, from the father. On the other hand, everything connected with flexibility of the soul or intellect comes from the mother. However, you can see an interesting difference only when you look at the entire spectrum of life, which you will find proven everywhere. There is a tremendous difference related to the child's sex. We can use Goethe's words to describe the wonderful relationship of the son to the mother and father:

> From Father I have stature,
> For the seriousness of life,

That is, everything connected with the interaction of the human being with the outer world.

> From Mother a happy nature
> And a love for storytelling.[3]

That is, the entirety of mental life. If we now look at the daughter, we see a quite different situation. The father's characteristics appear in the daughter in a way that raises them a step

---

2. Arthur Schopenhauer, *The World as Will and Idea*, ch. 43, "Inheritance of Traits," originally published in Berlin, 1894.
3. Wolfgang Johannes Goethe, *Zahme Xenien* (Gentle satires), volume VI, No. 32.

above the nature of will impulses, raises them to something ensouled, so that they address more the interaction with the environment. Of course, we do not find it everywhere, but in the daughter we can find, ensouled, the characteristics of a father who always acts courageously, who takes an enthusiastic interest in all kinds of things, and in this way has great interaction with the surroundings, expressing a kind of earnestness. In such a case, the daughter has a serious soul life. The characteristics of the father are so transformed in the daughter's soul that they make the daughter flexible where the father might be stiffer. The important characteristics that the father expresses outwardly we find more inwardly expressed in the daughter.

The father's character thus lives in the soul of the daughter, and the mother's soul characteristics, the intellectual agility as well as the talents and abilities that can be developed, live outwardly in the son. Goethe's mother was a woman who could tell stories and in whom fantasy functioned in a wonderful way. That was carried a step deeper in the son and became a tendency, a constitutional quality, so that Goethe the son could give humanity what lived in his mother. In this way, we can see how the son carries the mother's characteristics a step deeper so that they become a part of his constitution, whereas the daughter raises the father's characteristics a step so that they are more inward, more ensouled. There is perhaps nothing more characteristic of this than the difference between Goethe and his sister Cornelia. She was just like her father, with an inner stillness of soul and a serious nature, which allowed her to be the wonderful, extraordinarily good childhood friend Goethe needed. Remember that and then recall, according to his own description, that Goethe never had a good relationship with his father. That was because his father expressed the fatherly characteristics externally. Goethe needed these qualities, but could not understand them the way his father presented them. They were appropriate for his father, but because they lived in his sister's soul, she could be Goethe's good friend.

If you walk with me through history, you will see how at each step history confirms what I have said. We can find indications of historical confirmation everywhere. In this connection, we can find the most beautiful confirmation in the mother of the Maccabees, who sent her sons into death with heroic greatness because of what she and their forefathers believed. She expressed it thus

> I gave you your physical bodies, but the One who created humanity and the world gave you what I could not give. He will take care that you preserve it even if you lose your lives for the sake of your beliefs.[4]

We often find the motherly element presented in history, from Alexander's mother and the mother of the Gracchi,[5] right up to our own time. We see how the mother's characteristics arise, giving a person the necessary strength, talents, and constitution to act in the world. We could look at the stories of significant individuals everywhere in history and find the mother's characteristics so transformed that they have moved deeper and become capacities. Let's take the example of Bürger's[6] mother and his father, from whom he inherited his will characteristics.

---

4. 2 Maccabees 7:22–23. "You appeared in my womb, I know not how; it was not I who gave you life and breath and set in order your bodily frames. It is the Creator of the universe who molds man at his birth and plans the origin of all things. Therefore he, in his mercy, will give you back life and breath again, since now you put his laws above all thought of self." *The New English Bible with the Apocrypha,* Cambridge, 1971.

5. Roman tribunes, ca. A.D. 125.

6. Gottfried August Bürger (1747–1794), German poet, revived interest in folksong and a force behind German Romantic ballad literature.

He had little in common with his father, who was happy when he did not have to bother with raising his small boy. His mother, however, had a wonderfully flexible mind and the proper grammar and style so necessary for the poet. Because Bürger was a member of the next generation, he took these characteristics from his mother and made them effective. We could also think of Hebbel[7] and his relationship to his father. If you know Hebbel, you will find that all of his dry idiosyncrasies and peculiar interests resonate with what he inherited from his father. The old stonemason passed on much to his son. But, it was the mother and son who understood one another, and the mother protected Hebbel from becoming a stonemason in his home town, so that he could later give his dramas to humanity. It is very touching to read what Hebbel wrote in his diaries about the connection he had with his mother.

We can find numerous such examples. However, we should not conclude that things are false if we find something here or there that contradicts them, which would be the same as saying, "Physicists proved the law of gravity, but I can discredit it with all kinds of special situations." Laws of that sort do not exist to account for every possible circumstance, but to focus on what is important. This is what we must do in both the natural sciences and spiritual science; but we have not developed spiritual science to the point where it can proceed in the same way as natural science. If you consider this you will find the law of heredity I described confirmed everywhere. However, if you look at humanity as a whole you will see that what we call the human soul and the human constitution are not simple.

You could, of course, have an extreme desire for triviality and question how anthroposophists could have the audacity to

---

7. Christian Friedrich Hebbel (1813–1863), German poet and dramatist of Hegelian historical and moral tragedies.

separate the soul into three parts, and human nature into even more parts. You could say that we speak of a *sentient soul*, a *comprehension soul*, and a *consciousness soul*; but it would be much easier to speak of the soul as a unity that *thinks*, *feels*, and *wills*. This is certainly simpler, even more comfortable, but it is trivial. At the same time, it is something that a systematic consideration of the human being cannot accept in truth. The separation of the human soul into its component aspects does not arise simply from a desire to divide and create words. The sentient soul is the part of the soul that first meets and receives perceptions from the environment. It is also the part of the soul where desires and instincts develop, and we should separate it from the part where, in a certain sense, we process what we have gained. The sentient soul is active when we confront the external world and perceive its colors and tones, but it is also active when things arise that most people do not have under control—that is, our urges, desires, and passions. When we withdraw into ourselves and process all the perceptions, and so on, that we have received in such a way that we transform into feeling what the external world has stimulated in us, we live in the second portion of the soul, in the comprehension soul. Finally, to the extent that we direct and guide our thoughts and do not allow ourselves to be led about on a leash, we live in the consciousness soul.

In my books *An Outline of Occult Science* and *Theosophy*, you can read about the many different connections between these three aspects of the soul and the external world. These aspects do not exist just because we enjoy dividing things, but because what we call the sentient soul and consciousness soul each have a very different relationship to the cosmos.

The consciousness soul isolates human beings and allows them to perceive themselves as inwardly self-contained. What we call the comprehension soul brings the human being into a relationship with the environment and the entire cosmos and provides human beings with an understanding that they are essentially an extract or condensation of the entire cosmos. Because of the consciousness soul, human beings live within themselves, isolated. The human capacity that develops last—that is, logic and forming opinions, thoughts, and so on—is mainly experienced through the consciousness soul. The consciousness soul contains all of these. And with regard to these characteristics, the individual human essence that enters earthly existence through birth, indeed, tends most toward isolation. This innermost human essence develops last. Whereas the physical constitution develops first, a person's actual individuality develops last. Even though people were different in the past, however, and will also be different in the future, at present they develop opinions, concepts, and ideas in the most isolated portion of their being. These things influence a person's total personality least and appear only after the personality stabilizes following its plastic development.

Here we can see how human endowments develop along a specific path. We see first how the least isolated and least separated human aspect lives in the sentient soul, the soul of desires, which also has the greatest power to act on the whole human constitution. Because of this, when the sentient soul is working most intensively to form the child from within, we are least able to reach that child with opinions, theories, or ideas. We can best reach children by allowing the sentient soul to act. I presented this in my essay "The Education of the Child in the Light of Anthroposophy." You need to pay attention, especially in early childhood, not to the development of theories and rules, but to making sure the child *imitates,* and that you *live* what the child is to imitate. This is particularly important because the desire to imitate is one of the first capacities you can affect. Reprimands and rules are the least effective during that time.

Children imitate what they see because they necessarily develop according to how they are connected with their surroundings. We can form the first foundation for the entire personal essence of a child if, during the first seven years of childhood, we live what the child should imitate, after we have properly conceived of how we should act in the child's presence. For many people, this is, of course, a very strange principle of child rearing. Most people would ask how a child should behave, but anthroposophy comes along and says that adults should learn how to behave in front of children, even in words, attitudes, and thoughts. Children are much more receptive in their souls than people commonly think, and certainly more receptive than adults. There are people, no doubt, who have a certain kind of sensitivity and immediately notice when someone comes into a room and ruins the previous good mood. Even though people today notice little of this, it is particularly strong in children. What you do in detail is less important than the kind of person you try to be and the thoughts and ideas you carry. It is not enough to hide things from children while allowing yourself thoughts not intended for them. We must have and live the thoughts that we feel could and should live in the child. This is uncomfortable, but nevertheless true.

After the change of teeth begins, we can start to build upon authority—that is, not to build upon what people do, but upon what they harbor within the personality. During the first period of childhood it is most important that children imitate what we speak, do, and think. During the second period, it is most important that children feel they have someone they can count on and whose actions they can recognize as good. When children are between the ages of seven and fourteen or fifteen, we should not reprimand them with the intent of developing a sense of a moral theory in them, or of showing them that they should do one thing and not another. Rather we can best help

children if we can provide them with a feeling in the comprehension soul that what we do alongside them is good, and that
what we do not do, the child also should not do. All of this is
extremely important.

Only when children reach the age of fourteen or fifteen can
they develop the most isolated portion of their nature—that is,
the consciousness soul. Children can then work with and
develop their own opinions, concepts, and ideas. Children must
first stand on firm ground, however, and our task is to create it.
If we do not create such a firm basis by providing the opportunity through education for the child to freely develop as individuality requires, the child will then be overtaken by another
element—that is, a stiffness of the higher bodies. We can see
that in the way the child's eternal individuality fails to act on her
or him. The child becomes instead a slave of the physical constitution that encumbers people from outside. We can see this in
the way people fail to become the rulers of their spirit and soul,
and instead become completely dependent on the structures of
the body and soul. The character of such people is rigid and
unchangeable. On the other hand, if we are careful to allow a
child's innate interests to develop as far as possible, then that
child retains a certain kind of mobility throughout life and
retains the ability to adapt to new situations. By contrast, in
the first instance, the child develops a rigidity of body and
soul, which is maintained throughout life. We live in a time
when people have little value for human individuality, which
leaves us with little opportunity to realize that an older person
can still be mobile and lively, can still find the way to new
truths in new situations. Here we can see the way many people
relate to life.

Many people, once they have understood a particular world
view and become convinced of its truth, try to convince others
of its validity. When they clearly understand something, they

believe it is praiseworthy to bring this conviction to others. However, this is simply naïve. Our opinions do not depend at all on what is proven logically to us, or that is rarely the case. People's opinions and convictions arise from a very different place in the soul—from the will and the feeling. People can thus very well understand your logical discussions and comprehend your clever conclusions. Afterward, however, they do not at all accept them simply because what they believe or recognize as true does not arise from logic or intellect, but from the totality of their personality—that is, from those areas where will or feeling arise. Our thoughts are the last of our capacities to develop, long after our physical development is concluded. Thoughts are in the most isolated area, where people are least approachable. We can achieve more if we work with the deeper parts—with feeling and will—where we can still affect a person's constitution. However, when someone grows up in a very materialistic atmosphere—that is, where only matter has validity—then a number of feeling and will impulses develop that sculpt that young person's physical body, including the brain. Later, such a person can well understand good logical thinking, but it has no effect on the formation of the brain. Logical thoughts have the least effect on the human soul and, therefore, it is particularly important that we find our way to other human beings through the soul, not just through logic. If someone's brain has developed in a particular way, then logic can no longer reform it, because once the brain has become physical, it always reflects old ideas. We cannot possibly hope that world-views such as spiritual science, built on the purest kind of logic, will have any affect on people if we attempt to convince them. One who understands the spiritual-scientific impulse and believes it is possible to convince someone else about it through discussion or logic is the victim of illusion and grave error. In our age, there are many people—due to the totality of their personality, the nature of their will and feel-ing—who cannot see the reality of the spiritual world and spir-itual research. Out of the great number of people living around us, some are drawn toward spiritual science and have a vague feeling for it in the soul. Choice about one's world-view can occur only when it is comprehended through logic and human consciousness. A spiritual scientist knows how to approach people and differentiate between them. In one case, we find those we could preach to for years, but who would never understand our ideas; we would have to bring things into con-sciousness. You could speak to the soul of such people, but what was said could not, with all the resources available to the soul, be reflected logically. Other people, however, are formed so that they can comprehend what spiritual science develops and demonstrates logically, and thus find what already lives in the soul.

This is how we must address the great cultural tasks of the present and future. We must recognize how a human being's whole personality relates to what it slowly absorbs of the truth, and to the things that must unite with the personality during development and education. We will value more highly the task of developing human spirit-souls when we also recognize how the spirit-soul is fundamentally the shaper, the sculptor, the artist of the body-soul. Then, we will place greater value upon pursuing the development of the spirit-soul—particu-larly in the years when we can reach it through education—so that it can become powerful in its effect on the body-soul and take control of it. We should be aware that people make many errors in this area. You can see from what I have presented how human preferences and so forth affect the formation of view-points much more than pure logic. Pure logic can speak only when desires and instincts are completely quiet. Until then, we need to be aware that when we believe we have developed a specific capacity, something we have left untouched will suddenly appear.

Suppose we raise a child by emphasizing only the capacity for abstract thinking, as is so often done in school. Those pure concepts and abstract ideas cannot affect the child's feeling life. The feeling life remains undeveloped and unformed, and this shows itself later in all kinds of ordinary experiences. Even in highly regarded people we often see two different natures. If they have been unable to develop what lies deeper within their personality, then things such as preferences, tendencies, and sympathies often appear in very different ways. Every student has experienced standing before professors who have a good understanding of their fields, and how a one-sidedness is expressed by a preference for answers stated exactly as they want to hear them. Woe to the students who do not understand how to clothe their answers in words the professors want to hear!

Moriz Benedikt's book on psychology says much that is true about the mistakes made in education. He gives, for example, the case of two students standing for examinations before two professors. One student answered the questions as the other's professor would have wanted them answered. Had he given that professor his answers, he would have passed the examination with flying colors. For the other student, the situation was exactly the reverse, and thus they both failed.

We can see from this how well we can clothe unassailable facts in logical forms. As teachers, however, if we cannot clothe our concepts within our teaching of the subject matter, we will be unable to find a suitable way to develop the child. The question is, how should we relate to another person? During the primary developmental years we should approach children as little as possible with abstract concepts and ideas, which are ineffective, but rather with ideas that are as pictorial as possible. This is why I have emphasized that concepts should have a pictorial quality, that we should present concepts pictorially or in images. Concepts received as pictures or images, or even fantasy, have considerable strength to affect our physical constitution. You can see how a pictorial quality in things affects our constitution when you realize how little it helps to tell someone who is ill to do this or that, or not to do something else. This all helps very little. However, you can place an apparatus nearby that looks electrical, for example, and give the patient two handles to grip; even though you allow no electricity to pass and the patient has only an image and feels no electricity, it will still help. Whenever you hear it claimed that the power of suggestion plays a large role, you should be aware that it is not just any power of suggestion, but one that is pictorial.

In our age, it has slowly become the custom to give little attention to the spiritual-scientific principle that children can only begin to develop concepts and ideas between the ages of fourteen and twenty-one, and that during that time we should give them concepts they will develop only later. We now consider instead that children are old enough before the end of that period to write newspaper articles or editorials, which are then printed and accepted by the public. It is difficult to keep abstract concepts distant until that time and to direct children's attention only toward what is pictorial. Pictorial concepts have the power to affect the body-soul constitution.

You can find this confirmed everywhere, but people pay no attention to it. For instance, Moriz Benedikt complains about how clumsy so many prep school students are later in life. This is because their education was so void of description. Education has very little interest in being descriptive and uses only abstract concepts, even when teaching languages. In contrast, even in our hands we can feel what is presented to us descriptively, because we meet the object itself through those pictures.

If you want to imagine an object, then you must move your hands in a circle or ellipse so that you can feel a connection to the pictured object through your hand. This is not just imitation, but feeling and learning to appreciate things shows us how pictorial images affect the limbs, making them flexible and limber. Many modern people, when they lose a button, are unable to sew on another one. That is a great disadvantage. We need to be able to act in the external world under all circumstances. Of course, we cannot learn everything. However, we can learn how things that exist in the spirit-soul can slip out of the spiritual and into the bodily soul, and thus make our limbs limber. No one who was taught, during youth, to feel what is external will become clumsy later in life, because what lies below consciousness can best affect our constitution. The same is true of speech. A language is best learned when one cannot understand its grammar, because one then learns with that part of the soul that belongs to the deeper layers.

Humankind and individuals have both developed in that way. On another occasion, I referred to Laurenz Müllner's remarks about Saint Peter's in Rome. He said that spatial mechanics are wonderfully expressed in a concealed way in the dome of Saint Peter's. He goes on to say that Galileo's soaring spirit later discovered the laws of mechanics that Michelangelo expressed in the dome, and that Galileo thus gave us the science of mechanics. I have also mentioned that the death of Michelangelo coincided with the birth of Galileo. Thus, the abstract laws of mechanics existing in the human consciousness soul were discovered after what had lived in the lower aspects of Michelangelo's soul was constructed in space. In the same way that higher aspects of the soul develop from the lower aspects, as individuals, we develop our limbs based on our constitution, and then we can look back and form concepts about them. People live in the midst of human society, submerged in an atmosphere that is the spirit-soul of our surroundings. What they bring with them into earthly existence is thus formed and developed. However, people bring into earthly life not just what they receive through heredity from the mother and the father; they also bring an untold variety of a third kind, determined by the eternal human individuality. The human individuality needs inherited characteristics, but it must absorb and develop them. That is even more important than what we bring into existence as our individuality. We enter earthly existence through birth, and there a creative and productive spirituality takes over the formative material of heredity before we can develop concepts. Only later is the consciousness soul added. This is how we can see the human individuality that sculpts capacities and talents. If we are to be teachers, then our task is to consider the spiritual riddle that we must solve for each individual human being.

All of this points to a particular attitude. When Goethe found Schiller's skull in a charnel house and saw how it was formed, how Schiller's individuality had worked on it, he realized that Schiller's fluid spirit must have acted to form his skull so that he could become what he became. Goethe expressed his thoughts with these words:

> What more can human life achieve,
> Than the revelation of God's nature,
> How substance dissolves into spirit,
> And how that born of spirit is solidly held.[8]

We need to understand Goethe's remark in the context in which he made it. Someone who would accept this remark

---

8. Johann Wolfgang Goethe, "*Im ernsten Beinhause war's...*," Weimar, 1890.

without recognizing that what is born from the spirit is imprinted on a solid form would not understand it. You would also not understand it if you did not know of Goethe's deep insight into the eternal weaving of the individuality that moves from birth to birth through reincarnation, which is the true architect of human beings.

Through a simple comparison, we can see how we receive our organs from the spirit, and how those organs are the spirit. A clock shows us the time, but we could not use it if time had not first formed the human spirit. We need our brain to think in the physical world, but we could not use it to think if cosmic spirit had not formed it. We would also not be able to form it individually if the spirit had not placed our individuality into our humanly formed brain. We can understand more deeply what I expressed today, and what Goethe meant when he indicated what determines all talents and capacities, if we understand the stars in the way we understand anything else in the world. We must understand what is active within human beings as something eternal that goes through the gates of death, only moving forward into new developmental stages. We can summarize what we have considered today through the mood of Goethe's thoughts in *Orphic Prophecies*:

> As on the day to the world you were given,
> The sun arose to greet the planets,
> Then you began your unfolding,
> In accord with the laws of your entry.
> So you must be, you cannot flee.
> Thus spoke the Sibyls, thus the prophets;
> And no time and no power can destroy
> The imprint that in life develops.

THE FOUNDATIONS
OF WALDORF EDUCATION

THE FIRST FREE WALDORF SCHOOL opened its doors in Stuttgart, Germany, in September, 1919, under the auspices of Emil Molt, the Director of the Waldorf Astoria Cigarette Company and a student of Rudolf Steiner's spiritual science and particularly of Steiner's call for social renewal.

It was only the previous year—amid the social chaos following the end of World War I—that Emil Molt, responding to Steiner's prognosis that truly human change would not be possible unless a sufficient number of people received an education that developed the whole human being, decided to create a school for his workers' children. Conversations with the Minister of Education and with Rudolf Steiner, in early 1919, then led rapidly to the forming of the first school.

Since that time, more than six hundred schools have opened around the globe—from Italy, France, Portugal, Spain, Holland, Belgium, Great Britain, Norway, Finland and Sweden to Russia, Georgia, Poland, Hungary, Romania, Israel, South Africa, Australia, Brazil, Chile, Peru, Argentina, Japan, etc.—making the Waldorf School Movement the largest independent school movement in the world. The United States, Canada, and Mexico alone now have more than 120 schools.

Although each Waldorf school is independent, and although there is a healthy oral tradition going back to the first Waldorf teachers and to Steiner himself, as well as a growing body of secondary literature, the true foundations of the Waldorf method and spirit remain the many lectures that Rudolf Steiner gave on the subject. For five years (1919–24), Rudolf Steiner, while simultaneously working on many other fronts, tirelessly dedicated himself to the dissemination of the idea of Waldorf education. He gave manifold lectures to teachers, parents, the general public, and even the children themselves. New schools were founded. The Movement grew.

While many of Steiner's foundational lectures have been translated and published in the past, some have never appeared in English, and many have been virtually unobtainable for years. To remedy this situation and to establish a coherent basis for Waldorf Education, Anthroposophic Press has decided to publish the complete series of Steiner lectures and writings on education in a uniform series. This series will thus constitute an authoritative foundation for work in educational renewal, for Waldorf teachers, parents, and educators generally.

RUDOLF STEINER'S LECTURES
(AND WRITINGS) ON EDUCATION

I. *Allgemeine Menschenkunde als Grundlage der Pädagogik. Pädagogischer Grundkurs,* 14 Lectures, Stuttgart, 1919 (GA293). Previously *Study of Man.* **The Foundations of Human Experience** (Anthroposophic Press, 1996).

II. *Erziehungskunst Methodisch-Didaktisches,* 14 Lectures, Stuttgart, 1919 (GA294). **Practical Advice to Teachers** (Rudolf Steiner Press, 1976).

III. *Erziehungskunst. Methodisch-Didaktisches,* 15 Discussions, Stuttgart, 1919 (GA 295). **Discussions with Teachers** (Anthroposophic Press, 1997).

IV. *Die Erziehungsfrage als soziale Frage,* 6 Lectures, Dornach, 1919 (GA296). **Education as a Social Problem** (Anthroposophic Press, 1969).

V. *Die Waldorf Schule und ihr Geist,* 6 Lectures, Stuttgart and Basel, 1919 (GA 297). **The Spirit of the Waldorf School** (Anthroposophic Press, 1995).

VI. *Rudolf Steiner in der Waldorfschule, Vorträge und Ansprachen,* Stuttgart, 1919–1924 (GA 298). **Rudolf Steiner in the Waldorf School**, (Anthroposophic Press, 1996).

VII. *Geisteswissenschaftliche Sprachbetrachtungen,* 6 Lectures, Stuttgart, 1919 (GA 299). **The Genius of Language** (Anthroposophic Press, 1995).

VIII. *Konferenzen mit den Lehren der Freien Waldorfschule 1919–1924,* 3 Volumes (GA 300). **Conferences with Teachers** (Steiner Schools Fellowship, 1986, 1987, 1988, 1989).

IX. *Die Erneuerung der Pädagogisch-didaktischen Kunst durch Geisteswissenschaft,* 14 Lectures, Basel, 1920 (GA 301). **The Renewal of Education** (Kolisko Archive Publications for Steiner Schools Fellowship Publications, Michael Hall, Forest Row, East Sussex, UK, 1981).

X. *Menschenerkenntnis und Unterrichtsgestaltung,* 8 Lectures, Stuttgart, 1921 (GA 302). Previously *The Supplementary Course—Upper School* and *Waldorf Education for Adolescence.* **Education for Adolescents** (Anthroposophic Press, 1996).

XI. *Erziehung und Unterrricht aus Menschenerkenntnis,* 9 Lectures, Stuttgart, 1920, 1922, 1923 (GA302a). The first four lectures available as **Balance in Teaching** (Mercury Press, 1982); last three lectures as **Deeper Insights into Education** (Anthroposophic Press, 1988).

XII. *Die Gesunde Entwickelung des Menschenwesens,* 16 Lectures, Dornach, 1921–22 (GA303). **Soul Economy and Waldorf Education** (Anthroposophic Press, 1986).

XIII. *Erziehungs- und Unterrichtsmethoden auf anthroposophischer Grundlage,* 9 Public lectures, various cities, 1921–22 (GA304). **Waldorf Education and Anthroposophy I** (Anthroposophic Press, 1995).

XIV. *Anthroposophische Menschenkunde und Pädagogik,* 9 Public lectures, various cities, 1923–24 (GA304a). **Waldorf Education and Anthroposophy II** (Anthroposophic Press, 1996).

XV. *Die geistig-seelischen Grundkräfte der Erziehungskunst,* 12 Lectures, 1 Special Lecture, Oxford 1922 (GA 305). **The Spiritual Ground of Education** (Garber Publications, n.d.).

XVI. *Die pädagogische Praxis vom Gesichtspunkte geisteswissenschaftlicher Menschenerkenntnis,* 8 Lectures, Dornach, 1923 (GA306). **The Child's Changing Consciousness and Waldorf Education** (Anthroposophic Press, 1996).

XVII. *Gegenwärtiges Geistesleben und Erziehung,* 14 Lectures, Ilkley, 1923 (GA307). **A Modern Art of Education** (Rudolf Steiner Press, 1981) and **Education and Modern Spiritual Life** (Garber Publications, 1989).

XVIII. *Die Methodik des Lehrens und die Lebensbedingungen des Erziehens,* 5 Lectures, Stuttgart, 1924 (GA308). **The Essentials of Education** (Rudolf Steiner Press, 1968).

XIX. *Anthroposophische Pädagogik und ihre Voraussetzungen,* 5 Lectures, Bern, 1924 (GA 309). **The Roots of Education** (Anthroposophic Press, 1997).

XX. *Der pädagogische Wert der Menschenerkenntnis und der Kulturwert der Pädagogik,* 10 Public lectures, Arnheim, 1924 (GA310). **Human Values in Education** (Rudolf Steiner Press, 1971).

XXI. *Die Kunst des Erziehens aus dem Erfassen der Menschenwesenheit,* 7 Lectures, Torquay, 1924 (GA311). **The Kingdom of Childhood** (Anthroposophic Press, 1995).

XXII. *Geisteswissenschaftliche Impulse zur Entwicklung der Physik. Erster naturwissenschaftliche Kurs: Licht, Farbe, Ton—Masse, Elektrizität, Magnetismus,* 10 Lectures, Stuttgart, 1919–20 (GA 320). **The Light Course** (Steiner Schools Fellowship,1977).

XXIII. *Geisteswissenschaftliche Impulse zur Entwickelung der Physik. Zweiter naturwissenschaftliche Kurs: die Wärme auf die Grenze positiver und negativer Materialität,*14 Lectures, Stuttgart, 1920 (GA 321). **The Warmth Course** (Mercury Press, 1988).

XXIV. *Das Verhältnis der verschiedenen naturwissenschaftlichen Gebiete zur Astronomie. Dritter naturwissenschaftliche Kurs: Himmelskunde in Bezeiehung zum Menschen und zur Menschenkunde,* 18 Lectures, Stuttgart, 1921 (GA 323). Available in typescript only as **"The Relation of the Diverse Branches of Natural Science to Astronomy."**

XXV. **The Education of the Child and Early Lectures on Education** (A collection) (Anthroposophic Press, 1996).

XXVI. Miscellaneous.

SᴇʟᴇᴄᴛᴇᴅBɪʙʟɪᴏɢʀᴀᴘʜʏ

Basic Works by Rudolf Steiner

Anthroposophy (A Fragment), Anthroposophic Press, Hudson, NY, 1996.
An Autobiography, Steinerbooks, Blauvelt, NY, 1977.
Christianity as Mystical Fact, Anthroposophic Press, Hudson, NY, 1986.
How to Know Higher Worlds: A Modern Path of Initiation, Anthroposophic Press, Hudson, NY, 1994.
Intuitive Thinking as a Spiritual Path: A Philosophy of Freedom, Anthroposophic Press, Hudson, NY, 1995.
An Outline of Occult Science, Anthroposophic Press, Hudson, NY, 1972.
A Road to Self-Knowledge and The Threshold of the Spiritual World, Rudolf Steiner Press, London, 1975.
Theosophy: An Introduction to the Spiritual Processes in Human Life and in the Cosmos, Anthroposophic Press, Hudson, NY, 1994.

Books by Other Authors

Anschütz, Marieke, *Children and Their Temperaments,* Floris Books, Edinburgh, 1995.
Baldwin Dancy, Rahima, *You Are Your Child's First Teacher,* Celestial Arts, Berkeley, CA, 1989.
Childs, Gilbert, *Steiner Education in Theory and Practice,* Floris Books, Edinburgh, 1993.
——*Understanding Your Temperament: A Guide to the Four Temperaments,* Sophia Books, London, 1995.
Edmunds, L. Francis, *Renewing Education: Selected Writings on Steiner Education,* Hawthorn Press, Stroud, UK, 1992.
——*Rudolf Steiner Education: The Waldorf School,* Rudolf Steiner Press, London, 1992.
Finser, Torin M., *School as a Journey: The Eight-Year Odyssey of a Waldorf Teacher and His Class,* Anthroposophic Press, Hudson, NY, 1994.
Gardner, John, *Education in Search of the Spirit,* Anthroposophic Press, Hudson, NY, 1996.
Heydebrand, Caroline von, *Childhood: A Study of the Growing Child,* Anthroposophic Press, Hudson, NY, 1995.
McAllen, Audrey, *Sleep: An Unobserved Element in Education,* Hawthorn Press, Stroud, UK, 1995.
Murphy, Christine, ed./trans., *Emil Molt and the Beginnings of the Waldorf School Movement: Sketches from an Autobiography,* Floris Press, Edinburgh, 1991.
Spock, Marjorie, *Teaching as a Lively Art,* Anthroposophic Press, Hudson, NY, 1985.

INDEX

DURING THE LAST TWO DECADES of the nineteenth century the Austrian-born Rudolf Steiner (1861–1925) became a respected and well-published scientific, literary, and philosophical scholar, particularly known for his work on Goethe's scientific writings. After the turn of the century he began to develop his earlier philosophical principles into an approach to methodical research of psychological and spiritual phenomena.

His multifaceted genius has led to innovative and holistic approaches in medicine, science, education (Waldorf schools), special education, philosophy, religion, economics, agriculture (Biodynamic method), architecture, drama, new arts of eurythmy and speech, and other fields. In 1924 he founded the General Anthroposophical Society, which today has branches throughout the world.